PATRIOT PRIESTS

PATRIOT PRIESTS

*French Catholic Clergy and
National Identity in World War I*

ANITA RASI MAY

University of Oklahoma Press : Norman

Library of Congress Cataloging-in-Publication Data

Name: May, Anita Rasi, 1940– author.
Title: Patriot priests : French Catholic clergy and national identity in World War I / Anita Rasi May.
Description: Norman : University of Oklahoma Press, 2018. | Includes bibliographical references and index.
Identifiers: LCCN 2017026924 | ISBN 978-0-8061-5908-9 (paper)
Subjects: LCSH: Catholic Church—France—Clergy—History—20th century. | World War, 1914–1918—Religious aspects—Catholic Church. | Priests—France—History—20th century. | Military chaplain—Catholic Church—History—20th century. | World War, 1914–1918—Chaplains—France. | Catholic Church—France—History—20th century.
Classification: LCC D622 .M325 2018 | DDC 940.4/780944—dc23
LC record available at https://lccn.loc.gov/2017026924

For Tom

CONTENTS

ACKNOWLEDGMENTS

The late John W. Bush, S.J., taught me to love French history as an under-graduate at Le Moyne College and invited me to my first meeting of the Society for French Historical Studies. My interest in the role of religion in the national life of France in the nineteenth and twentieth centuries began during my graduate studies under Seymour Drescher at the University of Pittsburgh. My first foray into the topic dealt with the quarrels between the bishops, the Catholic press, and the State during the July Monarchy and Second Empire. When I had the opportunity to return to research, after a career as executive director of the state program of the National Endowment for the Humanities in Oklahoma, my interest turned to the imminent centennial of the Great War. Already familiar with the essay of Joseph F. Byrnes on priests and schoolteachers in the war, I quickly discovered the work of Raymond Jonas on Claire Ferchaud and was intrigued to find a curious relationship between the characters and themes in my earlier work and those in church-state relations during World War I. Early conversations with Professor Byrnes and Professor Jonas as well as Martha Hanna helped me to focus my research.

My work would have been much more difficult without the support of colleagues at the University of Oklahoma's History Department, David W. Levy and Robert Griswold, and former Provost Nancy Mergler, who helped me obtain library privileges there. I also owe a debt of gratitude to the archivists at the Archives historiques de l'Archevêché de Paris, Abbé Philippe Ploix, and Vincent Thauziès, who helped identify many sources I would not have known otherwise.

I found the comments and encouragement of colleagues who participated with me or attended sessions at scholarly meetings especially insightful. They helped me to formulate new questions and identify new research material. These included: Nicole Hudgins and John Monroe at the Western Society for French History in Baton Rouge in 2010; Brenna Moore and Thomas Kselman at the American Historical Association in Boston in 2011; and Oscar Cole Arnal and John W. Hellman at the Society for French Historical Studies in Montreal in 2014.

Several colleagues and friends read and critiqued versions of this manuscript, including Seymour Drescher, Oscar Cole Arnal, Anne G. Lynch, Dianna Everett, and David W. Levy. Their suggestions helped to sharpen my focus. Conversations with E. Anthony Rotundo provided context for the priests' concern for "virile friendships" and manliness. Marilyn Sparks Severson assisted with my archival research in France and assured the accuracy of several translations.

But perhaps the two persons who were most supportive of my research and writing are my husband, historian-anthropologist, J. Thomas May (whose research into the wartime service of his father, James A. May, Sr., stimulated my own interest in the Great War), and my art historian daughter, Rose Marie May. They spent hours discussing, reading, and commenting on drafts. Without their unlimited encouragement, this project might never have come to fruition.

PATRIOT PRIESTS

INTRODUCTION

Some historians have described the mobilization of the French clergy as the great novelty of World War I. Military laws passed in 1889 and in 1905 provided for the drafting of seminarians and priests into military service. The first law promised that if war occurred, the priest would be assigned to noncombat duties; the second law increased the years of required service from one to two and eliminated the exemption from combat assignment. From a twenty-first century perspective, this conscription certainly appears to be a great anomaly, first because canon law specifically forbade the clergy to kill, and second because the priests, both diocesan and religious, had been increasingly marginalized from French society by the anticlerical policies of Republicans, determined to create a more secular state.

Nonetheless, resident parish clergy and seminarians immediately responded to the call to arms. Members of French religious orders, exiled during the Third Republic, hastened to return to France to take up their military duties. Even those who had been exempted or discharged from military duty volunteered to be chaplains in a service established by Count Albert de Mun, a Catholic deputy, in the opening days of the war. The bishops and superiors of religious orders gave their full support to both the conscripted men and the volunteers, and the Vatican provided special rules and dispensations for them.

Although this phenomenon has been described in various histories of the period, this study is the first to view the war through the lens of individual priests' experience. Their war narrative is unique and important for several reasons. It contributes to the understanding of the very human reactions to engagement in the Great War on the part of men who were schooled for the altar rather than the battlefield. It portrays, in very personal terms, the graphic experiences that transformed the relationship between the priests and the soldiers, enough to dissipate the century-long conflict between Republican secularists and the Catholic Church.

This book fits well within the new approach to the history of World War I that progressively developed since the mid-1970s, fostered by scholars such as Jean-Jacques Becker associated with the Centre de Recherche de l'Historial de Péronne. Becker explains that this new approach emphasizes what happened to the people who were "plunged mentally into a conflagration of an unknown dimension." He asserts that one can only comprehend the war through the "mental representations of contemporaries."[1] In keeping with this approach, I deemed it important to use lengthy excerpts from letters, war journals, and biographies. These were carefully selected and translated to allow for a deep understanding of the mental state of the priests.

The thirty-three priests whose memoirs and biographies I studied include twelve combatants, four government-appointed official chaplains, twelve noncombatants, volunteer chaplains, and stretcher-bearers or nurses who served in battles from Belgium to Verdun in Western Europe and in Salonika in the east. They graphically portrayed their feelings in their writings. They described their initial trepidation about their reception among their fellow soldiers and officers, which was somewhat allayed by their excitement at the opportunity to inspire conversions among unchurched men. But ultimately, as they passed through the crucible of a horrible war, they found their own humanity matched that of their comrades—their sense of being swept up in battle and the determination to continue fighting despite battle fatigue and to support their fellow soldiers. They found ways to redefine their priesthood in service to both comrades and families. At the same time the men who had never met a priest came to an appreciation of that same humanity, helping to dispel the suspicion that had grown up during the past years.

The combatants voice their struggle to maintain a priestly role despite their military duty. One Jesuit novice writes: "I find myself full of desires for an apostolate, but rather awkward. . . . I feel like a stranger to everyone, mistrusted by several, because I am a 'curé.' . . . Please God that I can at least give an example of the spirit of duty."[2] And others express astonishment at "the fierce joy" they experience when they kill and at the "intoxication of leading a company of picked troops under fire and taking a village."[3]

Some worry that it is a violation of the will of God for a priest to participate in war. Others are like the famous philosopher Pierre Teilhard de Chardin, who wrote to his cousin in 1917 after years of being a stretcher-bearer: "I assure you that I'd a thousand times rather be throwing grenades or handling a machine-gun than be supernumerary as I am now." He continued: "I feel that doing so I would be more a priest. Isn't a priest a man who has to bear the burden of life in all its forms, and shows by his own life how human work and love of God can be combined?"[4]

Those priests who survived the war experienced a profound sense of camaraderie and enjoyed a new appreciation from their fellow soldiers as they learned to serve believers and nonbelievers alike. Achille Liénart, later archbishop of Lille, writes in his journal: "May the resources of my priesthood, whose worth is more completely apparent to me, profit from the intimate knowledge of the popular soul acquired by the contact of all these days to glorify God more and to worthily serve France in peace."[5]

This book is the first to position the priests' accounts as a unique and important part of the narrative of World War I. It was inspired by and depends on the work of other historians, who have treated various aspects of the service of chaplains and priests in the war. Jacques Fontana provides a general history of Catholic attitudes in the war and includes a chapter on priests and their contributions. The early documentation of the work of the Bureau of Volunteer Chaplains provides an essential orientation to the question of chaplains in the war, while Xavier Boniface builds on that to provide a detailed history of the chaplaincy that focuses in one part of the book on the chaplains in World War I. These works are supplemented by articles by Nadine-Josette Chaline on chaplains as well as Joan Coffey's examination of the Saint Sulpice seminarians inducted after the first Military Law of 1889. Annette Becker and Raymond Jonas both treat the work of the chaplains, and Marie-Claude Flagéat analyzes the Jesuits' involvement in the war. Daniel Moulinet analyzed letters of priests and seminarians from the diocese of Moulins, mostly stretcher-bearers, who wrote to the superior of the seminary there. Joseph F. Byrnes describes the opportunities that the war service brought to reconcile priests with schoolteachers, who had come to see each other as archrivals in the prewar period. Alain Toulza, although a representative of the French right-wing Catholic heritage, provides a useful overview of priests' participation in the war and of the defense of their rights in the post-war period.[6]

Both Martha Hanna and Leonard Smith portray reactions to the war among the soldiers they studied, which are very similar to those of the priests. In Hanna's work on the letters of Paul and Marie Pireaud, she finds that both of them understand the horrors and harsh reality of the war, but continue to support the national war effort. Like the soldiers that Leonard Smith describes in *Embattled Self: French Soldier Testimony of the Great War*, these priests' memories and impressions do not fit neatly into what emerged in the twentieth century as the common narrative of the war, one that portrayed the soldier as tragic victim and the war as "futile."[7] Rather, the thoughts of the priests as they made sense of the war resonate with Jonathan H. Ebel's research findings that soldiers and chaplains in the American army found religious meaning in the war. As he explains, their testimonies allow us to reflect on the relationship between religion, violence, and citizenship.[8]

The strange embrace of war by a clergy who should have been dedicated to peace reflects a widespread view of war that prevailed at the turn of the century. George Mosse called it "a war mythology," shared on both sides of the Atlantic, which asserted that only war could transform callow youth into men of noble, chivalric resolve, save the nation from degeneracy, and restore its virile tradition. The studies of Ebel and Raymond Jonas also confirm a growing concern over the degeneracy and feminization of the Belle Époque and the conviction that the pleasures and intellectual life of the period were feminizing society.

This concern about feminization permeated both secular and religious society. Indeed, French Nationalists blamed their country's defeat in 1870 at the hands of the Germans on this growing effeminacy. They called for a "remasculinization" of the culture, which ultimately could only be proven in victorious war against the Germans. The French clergy also were concerned with the dwindling numbers of men who attended church. Complaints about the "feminization" of religion were frequent in the prewar period. In fact, there were those in the broader society who saw the very fact of a celibate priesthood, men dressed in skirts, as symbols of the feminine nature of religion. So in some sense, the war was seen as an antidote to "feminized" Christianity.[9]

My hypothesis that the role of the Catholic priests in the war helped to deflate the century-long conflict between secularists and Catholics is well supported in the historiography as described in Etienne Fouilloux's article, "Première Guerre mondiale et changement religieux en France." He states that this fact cannot be ignored after the research of Jacqueline Lalouette, Corinne Bonafoux-Verrax, as well as the biography of Paul Doncoeur, who led the resistance to further exile of the veteran priests in the postwar era. Annette Becker's work also outlines the importance of the priest in memorializing the dead both during and after the war.[10] Frédéric Le Moigne's description of the friendship and respect fellow veterans showed for the bishops installed after the war testifies to the long-lasting effect of the priests' war service. Of the one hundred and fifteen bishops appointed after the war, seventy-nine were veterans and most had served in combat or as stretcher-bearers or nurses.[11] Joseph F. Byrnes also confirms in his book *Catholic and French Forever* that the cataclysm of the war brought Catholic and social leaders back into national life in a détente fostered in the exigencies of the war.[12]

This book is based on memoirs, journals, and biographies of priests who participated in the war. Twenty-four of them were published between 1917 and 1921. Several priests compiled their notes years later, like Léonce Raffin. Other priests were like Achille Liénart, who edited his notebooks after the war but only intended them for his family. A family member who is also a scholar edited and published them in 2008. Some are compilations of personal letters by friends and colleagues of men who died at the front or from injuries during the war. Although these thirty-three works do not constitute a "random sample" of priests' writings, they do portray the experience of priests and seminarians from a variety of different social backgrounds, combatants as well as noncombatants.

It is important to note that these thirty-three men never proposed to represent their colleagues' opinions, but only to explain their own experiences and impressions. They wrote for a variety of purposes: some to inform their friends, relatives, and colleagues; some to stay in touch with their superiors or former professors; and some to describe the reality of the front for a broader audience. The biographers often state they are writing to preserve the memory of the dead soldier priest or to inspire young people to dedication to duty.

I confirmed the authenticity of all of these memoirs and biographies by consulting an encyclopedic listing of priests and religious men and women who served in the war, published by the Catholic press group Bonne Presse, entitled *La preuve du sang: Livre d'or du clergé et des congrégations* in 1925–30, and Jean Norton Cru's bibliography of combatants' accounts of the war entitled *Témoins: Essai d'analyse et de critique des souvenirs de combattants édités en français de 1915 à 1928*, published in 1929.[13] I have been able to confirm all but one of the men using these sources. The exception is René Gaëll (formerly René Estoffe), a hospital worker who wrote under the name Gaëll during the war. Contemporary sources as well as later historians cite his war stories.

Letters and correspondence in collections in the Archives of the Archdiocese of Paris and in the Archives of the Army, published collections of letters compiled during the war, and quotations from priests' letters in newspapers provide an important context for understanding the priests. Accounts in the contemporary press and in publications circulated to priests during the war, such as those in *Le Prêtre aux Armées*, also provide context but are less helpful because they fail to describe the experiences of particular individuals. Memoirs and collected letters of soldiers and officers were useful to understand other soldier's reactions to war and to the priests' participation.

The total number of priests in the war has never been verified by the military. The editors of the Bonne Presse undertook to gather names and service records from the military and from the dioceses. They admit that their count for *La preuve du sang* includes only priests and seminarians who served as chaplains, nurses, and stretcher-bearers who received military citations or decorations, or were killed, leaving out others who were merely combatants. The total for these priests was 33,211. Of these, 23,418 were from the dioceses and parishes of France and 12,554 were members of religious orders.[14]

To tell the story of the odyssey of French priests in World War I, I open with a chapter that describes the deterioration of their status during the nineteenth century. This context helps define the significance of the transformation that they and their fellow soldiers experienced during the war. During the thirty years prior to World War I, both Republican secularists and intransigent Catholics fed the growing animosity that resulted in anticlerical laws, which fell hardest on the priest. A journalist writing in the *Revue des Deux Mondes* in 1892 described the plight of the parish priest as "banished from the school, excluded from the committee directing official charities, regarded with malicious distrust or jealous hatred by the mayor and the schoolmaster, kept at arm's length as a compromising neighbor by all the minor officials employed by the commune or the State, spied on by the innkeeper, exposed to the anonymous denunciations of the local newspaper . . . he spends his mornings reciting prayers to empty pews and his afternoons planting cabbages and pruning roses."[15] Meanwhile priests in religious orders were exiled from France.

The anticlerical laws of the Third Republic are based on a concept of the separation of church and state that is very different from the American. Each is based on the history of the two countries. After centuries of abuse rooted in the intimate connection between the church and the state, the French intent is to protect the individual from the claims of religion. These are seen as inhibiting a citizen from freewill choice and burdening him with superstitious, unscientific beliefs. In contrast, the American concept was devised by people escaping religious persecution for not adhering to the religion of the state. Its intent is to protect all churches from state control and prevent the state from establishing one religious denomination as the state religion.[16]

In the following chapters I then turn to the witness and memory of the priests themselves to describe their experience of the war. They articulated their hopes of pursuing an apostolic or evangelizing mission in the midst of the war. After years of serving an increasingly feminine and middle- and upper-class population, they were excited about the opportunity they would have in the barracks and in the trenches to influence men that they would never have had a chance to meet. To some degree, they all saw it as a compensation for being in the war, but the combatants believed it exonerated their role in the fighting.

As priests described their war experiences, they explained their patriotism, their sense of belonging to France as well as to the church. They found ways to explain the war to themselves in terms of Christian values of sacrifice and abnegation, but some saw no conflict between Christian ideals and the ideals of this war against Germany. In any case, they never questioned their identification with a country that had marginalized them.

Progressively they found themselves among men who accepted them as they adapted their traditional role of pastor to the exigencies of war. These priests who had served fewer and fewer men worked out ways to reach and to serve them in the battlefield and found an acceptance they had lacked for a long period of time. There was a growing sense of dependency on the priest on the part of many of the soldiers and a sense of comradeship and appreciation between the priests and the soldiers, even those who were not devout Christians. And finally, in the postwar period there emerged a new relationship between the priests and the people due in large part to the memory of the priests' wartime service and to their key role in memorializing their many fallen comrades. This newly won respect provided the atmosphere in which both the government and Church leaders worked out compromises in their ongoing relationship.

This story of the French priests in the military is a story that brings a different memory of war into sharper focus and at the same time elucidates a milestone in church-state relations that in large part is unique to France. It provides a further exploration of the relationships between religion and war, as men who were schooled to value peace found identification with their fellow soldiers and with their country through participation in violence. They were attracted and repelled by the demands of the war. Theirs is a very unique human story as well as a story of institutional significance.

CHAPTER ONE

THE ANTICLERICAL
THIRD REPUBLIC

By August 1914 when World War I began, French priests were already pariahs in their own country. Parish clergy had lost both their official position as state functionaries and their state salaries when the National Assembly passed the law separating church and state in 1905. Members of religious orders lived in exile because of earlier laws prohibiting them from living in their communities. Although priests' influence had risen and fallen during the nineteenth century, it had waned nearly completely by the time the first guns sounded. This chapter outlines this decline, to set the stage for the story of priests and members of religious orders during World War I. I do not intend to reinterpret what some historians have come to refer to as "the culture wars" of the nineteenth century.[1]

The Concordat that Napoleon had negotiated with the Vatican in 1801 had stabilized the relationship between church and state in France, but increasing secularization and the growing popularity of science and participatory government disturbed it. In this atmosphere, the Catholic Church and its priests seemed unable or unwilling to adjust to modern conditions. During the Third Republic, established after the German victory in the Franco-Prussian War of 1870, the struggles became dominant in the national political discourse.

Writing in November 1879, Abbé Arthur Mugnier, a Parisian priest who was popular in fashionable circles and among the literary and intellectual elites of Paris, recognized the impact of political differences. He despaired over the increasing separation between the priest and the people of France: "We priests are fatally chased from everywhere, from the Parliaments, from the Academies where not one priest has a seat, from the foyers of the theaters where we are portrayed in the worst light. . . . Oh! I am more than ever devastated by the unbelievable rupture between intelligent Republicans and us. Why haven't we tried to reconcile with these admirably gifted men, who now declare themselves by word and pen our irreconcilable enemies?"[2]

Abbé Mugnier's description implies a fall from grace, from a privileged position in French society. And indeed, the Concordat had effectively restored the Catholic Church after its decimation during the French Revolution. Bishops and priests became officials of the French government and Catholicism was designated "the religion of the majority of the French." But the government now controlled Church property, designated bishops for approval by the pope, and paid the salaries of the clergy. Bishops could not meet together to make decisions, nor could they respond to growing urbanization by redistributing or creating new parishes.[3]

The Concordat made possible a little more than one hundred years of uneasy peace, which varied depending on the policies of the government in power. The Bourbon Restoration (1815–30) increased Church privileges, and the July Monarchy (1830–48) curtailed them. The Second Empire (1852–70) helped the Catholic Church to reach the height of its success in the nineteenth century. During its reign, the bishops enjoyed greater prestige and influence than prefects in the administrative departments of the nation, religious orders increased in numbers, church schools enrolled 40 percent of the nation's school children, and even lay schools included religious instruction and displayed crucifixes. Charitable works and committees grew exponentially in the dioceses and parishes, and religious celebrations of first communions, marriages, and burials remained well rooted in social life. Pilgrimages and devotions inspired by miracles and led by clergy drew ever larger crowds. Catholic newspapers run by both laymen and clergy gave the Church the modern tool of mass communication.[4]

The Church's influence grew even more in the immediate aftermath of the Franco-Prussian War. Royalists won 400 of the 650 seats in the Assembly because they promised to sue for peace, while Republican politicians proposed to continue fighting.[5] The Royalists felt empowered by the initial enthusiasm for religion to begin building the Basilica of Sacré Coeur as a sign of repentance. Although they were unable to establish the Christian monarchy they would have preferred, they passed numerous pieces of legislation favorable to the Catholic Church. For the first time since the Concordat, Catholics established their own universities and conferred degrees; bishops sat on the Higher Education Council of the nation and priests on departmental councils. In turn, bishops and priests made no secret of their strong endorsement of the Royalist-dominated government, which seemed to them to be crucial to the welfare of the Church.[6]

When Republicans won the majority of seats in the Chamber of Deputies in 1879, they had clear evidence that leading Catholic politicians and bishops were negotiating with the Bourbon pretender, the Count of Chambord, for a restoration of the monarchy. Catholic priests had openly supported the Royalist cause during the elections. There were rumors that the Bonapartist Cardinal de Bonnechose, archbishop of Rouen, had urged the Royalist-leaning president of the Republic, Patrice MacMahon, to execute a coup after the Republican victory. Instead MacMahon abdicated and the Republicans began purging officials, including army commanders who were avowedly Royalist and Catholic.[7]

Catholics fueled Republican suspicions of their loyalty to France with continued support for the pope against the newly formed Italian state, which had confiscated all papal territory except the Vatican. The 1870 Vatican Council's declaration of papal infallibility provided another dramatic symbol of a growing centralization of Rome's authority over local churches.[8] In this atmosphere, Léon Gambetta, elected president of the Chamber of Deputies, felt justified to declare: "What is most to be feared is the clerical party; there is the enemy." And further, "It is rare indeed for a Catholic to be a patriot."[9]

Earlier, Pius IX had literally gone to war against secular and modern society. Reacting against the Revolutions of 1848 in Italy and the loss of papal territory, he issued the *Syllabus of Errors* in 1864. He condemned a long list of "modern errors," including rationalism, liberalism, the denial of the papal right to territory, and religious tolerance as well as socialism, communism, and secret societies. As they prepared their case for the separation of church and state by the end of the century, Republicans like Georges Clemenceau still used the *Syllabus* to classify the Church as the enemy of the Republic. Speaking in the Senate in October 1902 he compared "the spirit of the French Revolution, expressed in the Declaration of the Rights of Man" with "the counter-revolution of the Roman Church, whose formula is the *Syllabus*."[10]

Republicans were further concerned that religious devotional practices were increasing, despite flagging routine church attendance. Historian Eugen

Weber asserts men who would not go to mass would make a pilgrimage. He says the peasantry was looking for miracles and the priest was expected to perform them—that is, curing animals, keeping crops safe. Thomas Kselman fully describes the dramatic rise in the number of pilgrimages to religious shrines. Although missionaries often staffed the shrines, they became more important to pastoral work as the nineteenth century progressed. Local priests generally became involved quickly in local miracles. Bishops investigated alleged miracles, but in most cases they were inclined to believe. Searching for ways to position itself against the rising tide of secularization, the Catholic Church embraced the miraculous with the willing cooperation of some civil officials and in response to popular demand.[11]

Catholic success in education was also a particularly egregious problem for Republicans. Both Church and government leaders felt that education held the key to shaping the social and moral state of the country. By the 1870s 40 percent of school children were in secondary schools taught by religious orders as a result of the Falloux Law of 1850, which allowed parents the right to choose a religious education for their children.[12] Wealthy bourgeois families were especially attracted to schools run by the religious orders, partly because of their concern for social standing. They wanted their sons to emulate and associate with the sons of aristocrats. However, even public schools included religious instruction and were often staffed by nuns.

Despite the Catholic Church's dominance in education and the revival of popular religious practices, there is much evidence that priests were losing their prominence in French communities. According to numerous authors, priests were often portrayed in local proverbs and popular lore as "money-grubbing" for charging fees for their services.[13] Husbands resented priests' influence over their wives, particularly over issues regarding birth control. Priests, who condemned dancing and drunkenness and other lapses in public morality, fanned the resentment.[14] Roger Magraw's study of the Department of the Isère concluded that parochial squabbles rather than national issues motivated anticlericalism. Mayors protested the priests' interference in local administrative matters and citizens complained that the clergymen were trying to control the mayors. They quarreled over the placement of new cemeteries and expenses for rebuilding churches and improving the priest's house. As tensions grew, citizens often demanded that the bishops remove the offending priests, and usually the bishops refused.[15]

A young parish priest in French Flanders, Abbé Jules-Auguste Lemire, asserted that priestly behavior fostered distrust, if not scorn. He encouraged his colleagues to pay greater attention to the plight of the poor, to practice frugality and mortification. He also criticized the interventions, often "heavy-handed," that the clergy made on the private life of the faithful.[16] He wrote: "A priest for most of the people (even believers) is a man who has nothing to do, who drinks wine every day and never misses dinner. How many times have I heard some honest peasants say: 'At twenty-five years old he has nothing more to fear or to even desire, while for us, always work, always fatigue, always brown bread, lime blossom tea, and pork. These are the gentlemen, the lords, the bons vivants.'"[17]

Both historians and contemporaries attribute the growing isolation of the priest, particularly among men, to the widespread decline in routine religious practice. Abbé Mugnier complained: "We say today, with our eyes full of tears: the men have gone away, the men have gone away! But the women remain and I assure you that they are very good at making the clergy, young and old, lose the best part of their intelligence and their time."[18] Others, however, claim that adherence to the Catholic Church before the Revolution was never as universal as was supposed by the clergy and the bishops in the nineteenth century. Historian John McManners refers to the practice of religion before the Revolution as "gregarious," that is, required by social norms. Some people went to church out of fear of reprisals or discrimination by local authorities, while during the Third Republic others turned away from religious practice for similar reasons.[19]

Urbanization and industrialization fueled this decline in religious practice, which historians refer to as de-Christianization. As more people moved away from their families for required military service or factory work in the cities, they had fewer opportunities or support for religious practice. Children, however, attended mass frequently as they prepared for the *communion solennelle* (solemn communion). They received extensive religious instruction for the first and probably the last time. As late as the 1890s, the event remained an important social celebration for families in many areas, marking the time that children from the "manual class" left school for work.[20]

The Catholic Church itself aided the process of de-Christianization by failing to educate priests who could deal with modernity. They were taught nothing to help them answer "scientific" arguments against religious doctrine.

Instead, seminarians read Joseph de Maistre, the champion of medieval revival. In a country that had established republics three times by means of revolutions, they studied Bishop Jacques Bossuet, a seventeenth-century advocate of absolute monarchy. Most priests went first to minor seminary, where they only mixed with other students intended for the priesthood. Their school atmosphere emphasized discipline and pious devotion. In the next phase of their curriculum in the major seminaries, they focused on moral theology, dogma, and philosophy. Some of the books used were new editions of those written in the eighteenth century.[21]

Even though there was evidence that the influence of the Catholic Church was waning, when Republicans took control of the Assembly in 1879 they were convinced that to secure the Republic they had to diminish, if not eliminate, the Catholic Church's control over education. They believed that, after all, education was the foundation of the Church's influence in the country. It was in the schools that the Church imprinted on young people a residual respect for religion, if not strict observance of religious practice. They firmly believed that religious education did not form patriots but rather encouraged loyalty to monarchical government and to an international organization, the Catholic Church, based in Rome. Gambetta called monks and nuns "a multicolored militia without a fatherland."[22]

Thus in February 1879 the Republicans initiated the nearly thirty-year pursuit of anticlerical policies that ended with the French government's unilateral breach of the Concordat with the Vatican, the separation of church and state. Their policies not only accelerated the process of de-Christianization but also served to further isolate the priest from French society. Although moderate voices periodically emerged above the fray during most of the years preceding the outbreak of the war, the positions of both the defenders of the Catholic Church and the Republicans hardened.

The newly victorious Republicans began their battle against "clericalism" with the Ferry Laws of 1880–81. These laws did away with the privileges recently granted to the Church in education. They removed bishops and ecclesiastics from national and departmental education councils, forbade the use of the term "university" by Catholic higher education establishments and took away their right to grant degrees. Further, they prohibited members of unauthorized religious orders (the French term is interchangeably *congrégations* or *associations*) from teaching at either private or state schools.

The Jesuits were a special target because they taught a large number of the officers who graduated from Saint-Cyr, the prestigious military college, as well as the children of prominent citizens from other privileged schools of higher education.

In the opinion of historian John McManners, the most far-reaching and successful effect of the Ferry Laws was the creation of "free and obligatory" primary education. Up to this time only nuns had taught girls, in private schools. By a decree of August 1879 each department was to have a "normal school" to train lay schoolmistresses to replace them. And in July 1880 an École Normale Supérieure was established in Paris as well.[23] Denominational instruction was formally banned in all state primary schools. Parents who wanted religious instruction for their children had to send them to the curé on Thursday afternoons. Nonetheless, middle-aged teachers, who were now supposed to teach "civil and moral instruction," did not easily scrap old formulae. In Brittany and the Massif Central they still taught the catechism and inspectors turned a blind eye. The new generation of teachers emerging from the École Normale Supérieure, however, was much more secular in orientation and allegedly helped contribute to de-Christianization.[24]

Jules Ferry, the ardent Republican who was responsible for these laws, became minister of public instruction in 1879 and continued in this office for four years. He intended to "modernize" the French education system, believing that the laicization of education was "this great reform which contains within itself all other reforms." It would be the "foundation of the whole democratic future," uniting Frenchmen in a common patriotism, preparing them to fight to recover Ferry's homeland of Lorraine from the Germans. He believed his reforms would help the poor, give women equality, and give factory workers dignity. They would rid the schools of clerics who "*dévirilise*" adolescents by teaching resignation, docility, and blind obedience.[25]

Ferry's pursuit of the religious orders, which had not been authorized by the Concordat, was deliberate and blatantly offensive to most Catholics. It caused the most reaction of all the anticlerical laws. The Republicans believed the members of religious orders were less controllable than parish priests. Unauthorized by the Concordat, they were multinational organizations, responsible only to the pope. The Ferry laws immediately dissolved the Jesuits but allowed other religious orders to apply for authorization within three months. In sympathy with the Jesuits, however, the others refused to apply.

The police then began to carry out orders of expulsion, which dramatized the law and made it seem unusually cruel.

Abbé Mugnier described going with a crowd of supporters to stand outside the Jesuit residence in Paris to watch the authorities evict the priests on June 29, 1880. He lamented that at the same time legislators were discussing amnesty for the rebellious Communards (radical and socialist-leaning rebels who had been deported for trying to establish a commune in Paris in 1871 after the French defeat by Germany).[26] In Paris, the Prefect of Police launched predawn raids on eleven houses of religious orders. In some areas of France people supported the raids, while in others people came out in sympathy with the monks, priests, or nuns. In some instances, monks who had served in the Franco-Prussian War came out in their uniforms with their military decorations.[27]

Additional laws promoted secularization and restricted the influence of priests and religious. These laws allowed Sunday work and gave mayors of communes control over religious processions and the keys to bell towers. They eliminated posts for chaplains in hospitals and public prayers at the opening of the parliamentary session. A law of July 27, 1884, restored divorce to the Civil Code, from which it had been removed in 1816. In addition, Republicans in government circles encouraged lay funerals and praised departmental prefects for removing crucifixes from state schools.[28]

In this same period, the National Assembly passed two laws that provide the basis for the role of priests in World War I: the law of July 8, 1880, abolished the office of military chaplain and the law of July 15, 1889, discontinued priests' exemption from military service. They were obligated for one year of service, rather than the usual three, and were promised that in case of war they could choose noncombat service.[29] Bishops immediately made their case against the conscription law, stating that drafting the clergy compromised both the clergy and the military strength of the army. Canon law forbade the spilling of blood and the precepts of the military did not teach the ideal of turning the other cheek. They argued that it was an abuse of the Concordat to require clergy to serve in the military because it restricted them from carrying out their religious duties. The prelates feared that their parishes and religious orders would be deprived of priests and that their seminaries would lose recruits. They also suspected that the Republicans were motivated by the belief that fewer men would be attracted to the priesthood if they could not avoid military service. Many bishops wrote to the minister of war, to senators and deputies, some spoke in Parliament, and some voiced their arguments in the press, but to no avail.[30]

Although politicians in both the Republican and Catholic camps took hard-line positions, the vast majority of nominally Catholic voters seemed immune to the struggle. They elected even more Republicans in 1881, demonstrating that their continued support for the Republic trumped their concern for church schools or religious orders.[31] Leo XIII, who became pope in 1878, realized that the Catholics were losing their battle in France against the Republican anticlericals. He believed that one of the reasons was that they had attached themselves to a losing cause by pushing the Royalist agenda. On February 16, 1892, he issued the encyclical *Au milieu des sollicitudes*, directed to the French bishops, clergy, and faithful. It stated that the Church is independent of all governments and cannot tie itself to any particular form of government. To make his point more firmly, he wrote directly to the cardinals on May 3, 1892, stating clearly, "Accept the Republic."[32]

His proclamations met less resistance than might have been expected because many Catholics were becoming disillusioned with the Royalists. As early as December 1880, Abbé Georges Frémont, a pro-Republican author and speaker, wrote that there was "a whole party of clergy" that wished to protect the Church by a rapprochement with more moderate Republicans. A number of bishops also were anxious to take the Church out of politics to save it from persecution.[33] After Leo's encyclical, some Catholics sought an electoral alliance with the Opportunists (a moderate faction within the Republican party), who wanted to cut ties with the more radically anticlerical left-wing Republicans.

Leo's directives ushered in several years of relative peace with no significant anticlerical legislation. The peace ended with the eruption of the Dreyfus Affair. The conviction of Alfred Dreyfus became the "Affair" when it was discovered that the letter implicating Dreyfus as a traitor had been forged. Initially most Frenchmen had believed that Dreyfus betrayed military secrets to the Germans, but once armed with proof of the forgery, his supporters began a campaign for a retrial. They were aided most flamboyantly by Émile Zola's open letter, "J'Accuse," which he published on the front page of his newspaper, *L'Aurore*, on January 13, 1898. He accused the government of anti-Semitism for falsely convicting Dreyfus of espionage.

Historians Maurice Larkin and René Rémond both allege that the Affair only exposed the underlying division that still existed between those who accepted Republican hopes for a humanity emancipated from "irrational" beliefs and those who felt that Republican policies were fundamentally detrimental to everything true and sacred in French tradition.[34] Some in Republican circles saw the Affair as an opportunity to recreate the Republican unity of former years around anticlericalism. The Socialists also believed they could advance their political influence. Although the bishops kept silent and some prominent Catholics spoke out in favor of Dreyfus, others joined the Catholic press, led by *La Croix*, to give the impression that every good Catholic was an anti-Dreyfusard. They claimed that a virtuous army was under attack by a conspiracy led by Jews and Freemasons. Count Albert de Mun, who often cast himself as the authentic voice of Catholics, echoed these sentiments in a speech to the Chamber of Deputies that met with thunderous applause and a vote to imprison Zola for treasonous libel.[35]

These virulent anti-Dreyfusard arguments in the Catholic press and in the Chamber of Deputies revived the old fear that the Republic was in danger from the clericals. When René Waldeck-Rousseau became prime minister in June 1899 his main aim was to restore public confidence by asserting government control over the army and the Catholic Church. He was afraid to take aggressive action against the army, so he dismissed or reassigned only a few army officers. Although raised in a devout Catholic family, he moved more aggressively to address the clerical problem. He thought he could do this best by crafting a new law on associations (religious orders).[36]

The religious orders, banned from schools in 1880, had slowly come back into France during the 1890s and resumed teaching in secondary schools. The Jesuits, accused again of training most of the graduates of the prestigious military academy, Saint-Cyr, would be the main target of the association law, but Waldeck-Rousseau also aimed for the Assumptionists. He believed their chief crime was "the venom they put into politics" through their national newspaper, *La Croix*, which reached half a million readers. Their propagation of anti-Semitism "under the image of Christ crucified" gave it "an insidious air of quasi-respectability," which other anti-Semitic advocates could never acquire. He also blamed them for undermining the attempted electoral alliance between Catholic and Republican moderates in 1898, a sentiment he shared with Leo XIII.[37]

Nonetheless, Waldeck-Rousseau sought a moderate law, which would restrict the power and influence of only these most problematic religious orders, the Jesuits and the Assumptionists. He assured the papal nuncio (ambassador from the Vatican) that he would not repeat the mistakes of 1880 by expelling all the religious orders and closing their schools. He knew the state could not afford to replace them. His bill would have allowed the administration the flexibility to authorize, by decree, the establishment of a particular order in one area and refuse it in another, where Republican sentiment was weak. But the legislative committee's final draft assigned authorization to the National Assembly.[38]

The bitter Dreyfus quarrels gave anticlericals a large majority in the 1902 elections, demonstrating one more time the relative indifference of Catholics to anticlerical policies. Appalled by the results, Waldeck-Rousseau resigned and left the implementation of the association law to Emile Combes, a virulent anticlerical. Many thought his animosity could be attributed to the fact that he had been turned down for ordination because he was too "proud." After leaving the seminary, he had become a doctor, a Freemason, and a convinced skeptic with regard to religion.[39] He believed that it was absolutely necessary for the wellbeing of the Republic to remove French young people from the influence of the clergy. As a result, he honored none of his predecessor's unofficial agreements with religious orders. Waldeck-Rousseau had promised all the orders that had received authorizations earlier that they would not have to reapply. These included the Sulpicians and Lazaristes, who taught in the seminaries; the Brothers of Christian Schools, who taught more than 200,000 children in primary schools; and more than three hundred orders of nuns. Instead Combes applied the law to all the religious orders, only authorizing orders of cloistered monks, missionaries, and hospital workers. The rest were rejected without hope of appeal.[40]

The law prohibited religious from living together in community in France and from wearing their habits. A large number of orders, including the Jesuits and the Franciscans, went into exile, transferring their communities to Britain, Belgium, Spain, and Italy. The members who remained dressed in civilian clothes and continued to teach in the schools or resumed their duties as nurses in hospitals. Those who tried to live together were prosecuted. Combes's measures closed down more than 10,049 primary schools by October 1903, but 5,839 reopened quickly, 3,858 of them staffed by secularized nuns and brothers.[41] Some 150,000 children were left with no school, and fewer than half of them were absorbed into the state system. A more specific law, passed in July 1904, prohibited members of religious orders from teaching in any school and ordered the closure of their schools, including their seminaries, within ten years. They were only allowed to train priests for overseas missions.[42]

Final separation of church and state was not far off. Although Combes personally agreed with earlier Republicans who believed it was better to maintain the Concordat as a means to control the Church, his left-wing supporters, including Georges Clemenceau and the Socialists, pushed him along. The Socialists, who had first seen anticlericalism as a capitalist plot to divert the attention of the working classes, now were pressed by their rank and file to support separation. Workers in the Departments of the Nord and the Aube were bitterly anticlerical, holding "civic first communions" with a diploma presented in the shape of a red flag, "civic baptisms," and meat teas on Good Friday, which was a fast day in Catholic observance. In the Nord, workers formed burial clubs to keep priests away from funerals.[43]

After more than two years of consideration, the National Assembly finally passed the law separating church and state and promulgated it on December 11, 1905. The law was to come into effect in a year's time. It proclaimed that the Republic recognized no religion nor did it pay the salaries of ministers, whether Protestant, Catholic, or Jew. Church buildings and property built before 1905 became the property of the state and local government. To be used for religious purposes, the property had to be under the control of newly created religious associations of laymen, who resided in the parish in question. If these associations were not established within one year of the law's implementation, the property would be allocated to organizations within the communes for charitable and public assistance.

Clerical salaries were to be phased out over four years and pensions were promised. The bishops would now be free to correspond with Rome and to adjust diocesan and parish boundaries. Religious emblems would remain in place and religious ornaments allowed in cemeteries, but a mayor could forbid "exterior manifestations," such as public processions, and would have decisive control over ringing church bells, with appeal to the prefect permitted.[44]

The law caused a great outcry in the Catholic press. Monarchists and nationalists saw it as an opportunity to attack the government and fully expected public resistance. Their hopes were fueled by protests in some rural areas to the inventories that the law required. Even in Paris mobs attacked police with stones and chair legs at the parishes of Sainte-Clothilde and Saint-Pierre du Gros-Caillou in February 1906. Although the bishops all discouraged violence, the outspoken opposition of the new pope, Pius X, encouraged it. He regarded the law as an affront, undermining the international standing of the papacy. Those who expected Catholic opposition to overturn the law, however, were proved wrong by the May 1906 election. Catholic and right-wing groups lost sixty seats and were reduced to 175 deputies.[45]

The bishops, for their part, were anxious to make an agreement with the government in order to maintain the resources to support the pastoral work of their dioceses and to reorganize the Church in France. As practical administrators who had much experience negotiating with prefects and local officials, they believed they would be able to keep Church property under their control without much difficulty even with the newly created religious associations. They were more afraid of chaos and financial disaster than they were of the schismatic competitors that some opponents envisioned.

Nonetheless, the pope forbade the bishops to work out a system of collaboration with the government. Despite the bishops' appeals after the May election, Pius X issued an encyclical, *Gravissimo*, published on August 10, 1906, that condemned the law and prohibited the formation of religious associations. He asserted that these associations could be formed under no circumstances without violating the sacred rights of the Church.[46] His refusal cost the Catholic Church nearly half a million francs' worth of property and the means of rebuilding new material resources. Only when the prohibition was lifted in 1924 could the Church undertake new building programs, but they never recovered what they lost in 1906. It took half the twentieth century and many bazaars and collections to replace these resources.[47]

The government was left with the dilemma of what to do with parish churches. Aristide Briand, by now the minister of public instruction and of worship, convinced his colleagues that it was best to leave the churches in the hands of the parish priests. He allowed presbyteries and bishops' palaces to be taken over by public authorities and put to various purposes. Some of the palaces became museums and some of the presbyteries were rented to the clergy, while some more indulgent mayors actually paid clergy to be caretakers of the presbyteries. The upkeep of the churches was the responsibility of the occupant unless the church had been listed as a historic and cultural monument. After a long campaign, the writer Maurice Barrès convinced Briand to place all churches built before 1800 on the list.[48]

The major problem the Catholic Church faced on a daily basis was the support of the parish priest. To solve this problem, the bishops initiated the *denier du culte* (fund for religion) on a diocesan basis to spare the priests the embarrassment of collecting for themselves. The funds were distributed equitably among the parish clergy. Collections varied by parish, richer parishes contributing more, and they fell off gradually between 1907 and 1910. To supplement this income priests were dependent on the fees they could charge for marriages, burials, and seat rental in churches, again demeaning their status with the public. In these circumstances the Church had trouble supporting its 42,000 clergy even at their former low salaries. At the same time, parishes were threatened by the decrease in the number of ordinations to the priesthood from 1,733 in 1901 to 825 in 1913, as parents discouraged their children from choosing such an uncertain mode of living.[49]

McManners asserts that the Separation Law, culminating as it did years of anticlerical legislation and propaganda, hastened the decline in religious practice. He states that Jean Vernant did the first technical statistical inquiry on church attendance and put it at only 2.4 percent in the Department of the Seine-et-Marne. In Limoges between 1901 and 1907 the number of births without baptism rose from 8 percent to 25 percent, of lay funerals from 6.85 percent to 22.9 percent, and of civil marriages from 18.5 percent to 48.5 percent.[50]

Nonetheless there were priests and lay people who saw the separation as an opportunity to orient the Church anew to vast sections of the society that had been outside its reach. The movements of Social Catholicism and Democratic Catholicism had been evolving over the past generation. Awakened to social problems in the 1890s by Leo XIII's encyclicals, priests helped create organizations to reach out to the working classes. Albert de Mun, although a Royalist who opposed Dreyfus and the Separation Law, had been the founder of the Workers' Circles and the Association of French Catholic Youth. As early as 1892 he proclaimed his vision of a new type of priest: "I would like to see in every French diocese a group of hand-picked priests, young and tough, with courage and initiative, who would study social issues and train themselves to talk about them to working-class audiences."[51]

When nearly seven hundred clergy, mostly parish priests, gathered in Reims in August 1896 to celebrate the fourteenth centenary of the baptism of Clovis, they called for certain reforms. In all their speeches, they voiced a clear recognition that the Church was alienated from the masses. They proposed a uniform catechism for all dioceses, simpler and more direct sermons, new methods of evangelization beyond church structures, and improved education for clergy. Some individuals proposed the relaxation of the rule about fasting for communion, which would be implemented at least on a temporary basis during World War I. One speaker actually regretted the existence of confessional schools that kept Catholic children in a compartment separate from the rest of the nation. And, on a prophetic note, another welcomed the conscription of seminarians as a chance to gain access, through the barracks, to social classes that never came near the curé.

The press on both the right and the left denounced the priest's congress, and the government forbade the use of ecclesiastical buildings for future assemblies. Many bishops agreed with the archbishop of Paris that the congress was "dangerous" because it was not under the leadership of the bishops. Rome too placed severe limitations on the subjects for debate at future meetings. Nonetheless there was another congress held at Bourges in 1900 where priests again urged new methods of evangelization in France, which they termed *un pays de mission* (a country of mission).[52]

While the separation was being debated, Abbé Lemire, foreseeing the economic problems, suggested that priests engage in hard labor, tilling the soil and so forth, in order to support themselves as St. Paul had.[53] After the separation, some priests did try to follow his suggestions. In the 14th arrondissement in Paris, Abbés Soulange-Boudin and Jean Viollet experimented with "social work" in the parish of Notre-Dame de Plaisance. Soulange-Boudin looked forward to the priest working all day and spending the evenings preaching in bars and cafés. Jean Viollet, who had been one of the few active Dreyfusards among the clergy, was enthused about the opportunities that would be possible for a poor priest. An Alliance of Worker Priests, formed a year after separation, soon gathered four hundred members. The bishops, however, worried that secular work would draw priests away from their regular pastoral duties, were not supportive and ultimately, the pope opposed it.[54]

Despite these long overdue attempts to address modern problems, by 1914 the Catholic Church in France had lost out in the century-long battle with secularization. The anticlerical laws had gradually cut off the routine access of priests and members of religious orders to the populace. The Separation

Law of 1905 had deprived churchmen of their official status as government functionaries and of their guaranteed, although low, salaries. Final disagreements had lost them access to Church property, even their own residences. Urbanization, industrialization, and the growing influence of science had all contributed to a decline in religious observance, exacerbated by the Church's opposition to most modern ideas. The Church was no longer the center of civic life, which had become strictly secularized, with public officials prohibited from attending church services in official capacities and bishops and priests not invited to civic events. Even at the level of family celebrations, more people were choosing secular marriages and burials. This left the priest as all but a pariah in French society, with influence over a very small minority of the population, mostly women.

Surprisingly bishops and priests, who were now so marginalized, responded willingly to the call of their country when war was declared in August 1914. Members of religious orders flocked back from exile and parish priests and seminary professors abandoned their posts to serve the nation. Bishops went out of their way to support the war effort in every way that they could even though they represented a religion that valued peace. Paradoxically the war provided the clergy with a new opportunity to adjust to the modern world and to the Republic, and to evangelize the working classes. The initial resurgence of church attendance, pilgrimages, and devotions renewed their hopes for a revitalization of the Church. Now the priests, volunteers, and conscripts would be thrust into the crucible of war, with all its contradictions to their religious duties and beliefs. They documented how they adapted, their motivations and experiences, their growth and change in their memoirs, journals, and letters, which are the focus of this book.

CHAPTER TWO

MOBILIZATION OF FRENCH PRIESTS

The Great Novelty of War

Despite years of anticlerical legislation, Catholics responded wholeheart-edly to the call for unity issued by the government at the beginning of World War I. They had a variety of reasons, both philosophical and practical. They believed the cause of France was "right" and "just" and they found reasons to hope for a restoration of Church influence, in the government's relaxation of anticlerical laws and in the initial manifestations of religious fervor among the populace.

The most remarkable sign of Church support for the war was the will-ingness with which the bishops and the priests themselves agreed to the mobilization of the clergy. But the complete lack of formal communication between church and state authorities served to complicate the role of the priest in the war. Whether he served in a noncombat position as a stretcher-bearer or nurse or chaplain, or as a combatant, the priest was subject to two different hierarchies, the military and the Church. He was left to sort out his role in the confusion of the battlefield, with conflicting loyalties and responsibilities.

His situation was also plagued by the latent suspicions rooted in the anti-clerical past. This chapter outlines the complexities and ambiguities inherent in the mobilization of the French clergy in World War I and in the priests' position in the war.

Catholic response to the French declaration of war on August 4, 1914, and to President Raymond Poincaré's call for a *union sacrée* (sacred union) removed all doubts about their patriotism. That patriotism was symbolized most dramatically by Count Albert de Mun, the outspoken Catholic deputy, who, when war was declared, crossed the Chamber of Deputies to shake the hand of Édouard Vaillant, the close associate of the slain socialist Jean Jaures. Vaillant, who had been one of the members of the Paris Commune, reached out his hand in turn for the first time to this former cavalry officer who had taken part in the repression of 1871. Théophile Delcassé, who had engineered the severing of diplomatic relations with the Vatican, saw De Mun's reaction and was moved to ask him if God would be with France. De Mun reassured him that God forgives and would answer their prayers.[1]

The hierarchy was not far behind. Cardinal Léon-Adolphe Amette, the archbishop of Paris, confirmed Catholic patriotism with his declaration: "We, Catholics, want to be the first to respond to the call of France."[2] Contemporary historian Abbé Joseph Brugerette asserted that despite the government's thirty years of "ceaselessly hindering its apostolic work," the Church could not do other than to rival the zeal and devotion of the rest of the country and work with all its power for national unity against the invader. He wrote: "As soon as the call for mobilization sounded, bishops and priests, women and men in religious orders forgot their well-founded grievances and had only one preoccupation, that of assisting the work of 'national defense' by all the means in their power."[3]

In his definitive book on Catholic attitudes toward World War I, Jacques Fontana states that French theologians, bolstered by the neo-Thomist theology of the seventeenth century, made the case for fighting for the "right." They did not deny that war is cruel and odious, but they asserted that this war was the inevitable result of the unreasonable ambitions of Germany. This was buttressed by a universal belief in France in the force of "right," in the crusade of the civilized, which was "eternal France." In fact, they were in perfect agreement with Frenchmen on the political left that France had to defend its soil and the "right."[4] Philip Jenkins's research also provides evidence that government leaders and the people in all the warring nations felt that their cause was just, that God was on their side—that this was indeed a "holy war."[5]

Catholic support for the war was also cemented by the conviction among some Catholics that the defeat of 1870 at the hands of the Germans was part of Otto von Bismarck's plan to limit France's influence in Europe and the Far East. In their opinion, Bismarck believed that the best way to do that was to decrease the influence of Catholicism and the papacy. For these Catholics the defense of the country was the defense of the Church itself, regardless of the "persecutions" under the Third Republic.[6]

Both the Catholic bishops and the press joined in firm support for the war. In their public statements, the bishops affirmed that France was fighting for justice and the "right" and they asked God for complete victory. They followed their words with actions. Although the Church had been dispossessed of its buildings as a consequence of the separation of church and state, the bishops offered the new buildings they had acquired to the government to be used as hospitals.[7] L'Écho de Paris, the Catholic newspaper that published Albert de Mun's regular columns, called pacifism a "criminal illusion" in its November 1, 1914 edition.[8] The widely circulated La Croix began calling the war a "crusade" and a "holy war" in articles between October 1914 and January 1915. In general, Catholics seemed determined to identify religion with patriotism.[9]

Some Catholics hoped that wholehearted support for the war would allow the Church to renew its influence over the people. They were convinced that the majority still had Christian convictions in the depths of their hearts.[10] This hope was buttressed in the early days of the war. From August 2, crowds throughout France were in front of the altars. Local officials, who had previously scorned the Church, encouraged men to clear their consciences as they went off to war, and allowed the distribution of religious medals and holy cards. Numerous pilgrimages were launched. Mgr. (Monseigneur) Alfred Baudrillart, rector of the Institut Catholique in Paris, proclaimed in La Croix, "In becoming again totally French, the national soul found itself Catholic again."[11]

Priests were astonished by the resurgence of religious fervor they witnessed. Abbé Pierre Lelièvre, a forty-year-old parish priest who would become a volunteer chaplain, described what he saw when he returned to his parish in the Ménilmontant section of Paris just after war was declared: "Very many men, who a long time ago had forgotten the way, have returned this morning to church. They resemble people who are suddenly waking up at the edge of an abyss, towards which they have walked for a long time without seeing it. The priests do not cease to hear confessions, to give absolution, to distribute rosaries and medals, and also to console."[12]

Priests suddenly began to experience a sometimes enthusiastic acceptance. Abbé J. M. Bourceret, a forty-four-year-old professor at Notre Dame des Champs in Paris, volunteered to be a nurse at the beginning of the war. He described that he heard "bravos, cheers, greetings, mixed with respect and confidence" as he bicycled across Paris with the insignia of the Red Cross on his cassock. He remarked: "With what ease people change their opinions: yesterday the enemy, today a friend, without any transition."[13]

Members of religious orders, returning from exile, had similar experiences. In February 1915 the *Revue du Tiers-Ordre* published an account of the welcome, which amazed and thrilled the Franciscans:

> You know the story of our return to France. It was a veritable triumph. In Paris, the spectacle was grandiose. We are twenty-five Franciscans, dressed in our religious habit, leaving the Gare du Nord. And the people cheer us: 'Bravo! Bravo! The monks! Hands stretch out to us, hands that yesterday would have been raised against us. At Étaples, I had to pass in front of 200 to 250 officers.... A tall young lieutenant stops me: 'Pardon, Father, are you a soldier?' 'Yes, lieutenant.' And I had to tell him where I came from, where I am going, and if I am happy to defend my country. Suddenly, the officers all surround me and applaud. There was a moment of surprise among all the travelers. But quickly they realize the reason for the demonstration. 'They are saluting the monk.'[14]

At the front, in the opening days of the war, religious fervor among both civilians and military men thrilled the priests. Abbé Bourceret was dispatched with his *ambulance* to the area of Verdun in August 1914.[15] He described chapels near Bar-le-Duc filled with women "bowed in reverence, which prevents them from being distracted from prayer. The gravity of the circumstances intensifies their piety, and in seeing them, I cannot bring myself to believe that so many hands joined in France will not vanquish divine severity."[16] The twenty-two-year-old Sulpician seminarian Cpl. Pierre Babouard rejoiced that five hundred soldiers, with their commander and several officers, attended mass at 3:30 in the morning on the day his unit left for the front. In his letter of August 4, 1914, he commented that many of the men who received communion that morning had not done so in a long time.[17]

The government backed away from its intense anticlericalism. Even before war was declared, on August 2, 1914, Minister of the Interior Louis Malvy, a radical Socialist, issued a dispatch to the prefects of all the departments that interrupted the implementation of the anticlerical laws. He suspended the execution of the decrees dissolving religious orders, the closing of their establishments, and in general all measures necessary to implement these laws. This allowed all the members of religious orders, men and women, to return to France to fulfill military obligations or to volunteer to help with the war effort.[18]

Nonetheless the spirit of anticlericalism was too entrenched to disappear completely. There were occasional outbursts even in the first days of the war, and more later. If some priests experienced remarkable acceptance, others like Abbé Lelièvre were motivated to prove their patriotism and their courage because of suspicion and insults. Lelièvre claimed that he answered the call of Albert de Mun for volunteer chaplains partly because of the epithets he heard on the street. He wrote: "A woman cried out: 'There is one who surely will not depart!' And another: 'Those priests will always profit from it, they bury the dead.'" He felt that he had to leave, although he preferred to die at home; he asserted that he certainly did not want to kill, but would go, to offer himself.[19]

Rumblings of anticlericalism were fed by the rumors, circulated soon after the declaration of war, that the clergy funded the war to pursue the Church's ambition for domination. It was alleged that the Kaiser himself had attended the Eucharistic Congress at Lourdes (a pilgrimage site) in July 1914, where the papal legate and the bishops gave him the treasury of the Grotto to help pay the cost of the war. There were also rumors that the Denier de Saint-Pierre (Fund for Saint Peter), collected for forty years by the Vatican, was given to the Germans. Some priests fanned these rumors with sermons describing the war as a punishment for France's irreligion.[20]

The most remarkable way in which the Church proved its loyalty was by wholeheartedly embracing clerical participation in the war. Bishops gave full support to the mobilization of their priests despite their worries about the depletion of priests in their dioceses and the spiritual well-being of the clergy. Mgr. Henri-Raymond Villard of Autun expressed the viewpoint of his colleagues in his pastoral letter of September 24, 1914, which stated, "In the past the Church gave its property to contribute to the defense of the *Patrie* (Fatherland), while the priests, who were not forced to shed human blood, were reserved for the peaceful sacrifice of the altar. But today, the Church has no more material riches; the only wealth it has is its clergy . . . in the face of the menacing oppressor, it is resigned to let them depart for the fields of battle."[21]

The conscription laws made it impossible, however, for priests to avoid mobilization. The military law of 1889 had allowed priests or seminarians to choose a noncombat position, as a nurse or stretcher-bearer, if war occurred. The military law of 1905 eliminated that exemption and increased the number of years a priest or seminarian had to serve from one to two. As a result, the youngest of the priests and seminarians, drafted in classes beginning in 1905, were assigned to combat. The 1905 law also decreed that men of twenty "classes," that is, years of induction, could be mobilized. It made twenty-five reserve divisions available from the beginning of World War I, which would mean that 8 million men would serve under the flag of France during the five years of the war.[22]

Despite the laws, one might have expected more opposition to the mobilization on the part of the bishops or the priests themselves, or at least that those members of religious orders in exile might have refused to return.[23] There were only a few lonely voices expressing doubt over bishops' allowing their priests to go to war. One of them was the prominent convert, novelist and essayist Léon Bloy, who wrote: "The soldier-priests! The cataclysm of impiety caused by Germany and the unpardonable cowardice of the French bishops made such a monstrosity possible. Twenty or thirty thousand priests, perhaps more, have been snatched from the altar and thrown among the combatants under the pretext of equality." He also lambasted the Catholic newspapers for their glorification of these "pretended heroes." But other prominent Catholic writers like Charles Péguy, who was killed at the front, gave the mobilization their full support and accolades.[24]

Statistics available for only thirty-five dioceses indicate the substantial disruption suffered in the dioceses of France. Extrapolating from these figures, it is estimated that between one-third and one-half of the parish priests were mobilized, leaving many parishes without a priest. This conclusion is substantiated by statistics, which established that 45,000 parish priests were serving dioceses in France at the time of the Separation Law and that 23,418 diocesan clergy served in the war.[25]

Albert de Mun declared eight days before he died, "C'est la guerre des prêtres" ("It is the war of the priests"). Priests were everywhere.[26] Indeed there were priests in combat positions, in the infantry, artillery, cavalry, and serving in the newly formed air force. Some of the older priests, who had received commissions during military duty before the war, returned to take their former rank and soon received promotions. The young seminarians from the post-1905 classes were soon promoted to officer status as well. Priests from the pre-1905 classes chose noncombat positions as nurses or stretcher-bearers, while many, not subject to mobilization, applied to be chaplains or to serve in any noncombat capacity. Missionaries, fluent in various languages, were often assigned to colonial troops or to the High Command to assist with communication.

Yet in the chaplaincy, where one would expect to find them, priests were fewest in number. As mentioned in the previous chapter, the peacetime chaplaincy had been eliminated in 1880 and the provisions of the decree of May 5, 1913, for a chaplaincy in time of war had not yet been implemented. Even so, that law prescribed only one priest for every ten thousand. In comparison, the United States and Canadian armed forces made provision for one chaplain for every one thousand men, the British one for every four thousand. At the beginning of the war, the French army selected and mobilized 100 *titulaire* (official) chaplains and 151 of them by 1915.[27] These were paid a salary by the government and held the rank of captain. By the end of the war, the total number of chaplains that had served in the French army during the course of the war was 1,500, while the British counted 3,475.[28]

This scarcity concerned Albert de Mun. Using the advantage of the recent demonstrations of unity, he approached Prime Minister René Viviani and made the case for the religious interests of families and the good moral effect that additional chaplains would make. He offered to organize volunteer chaplains and to be the intermediary between the Health Service and the bishops to recruit priests who were not subject to mobilization in the regular army. He promised that they would serve without pay, but would need to be given safe conduct to the territories occupied by the armies. Viviani agreed to the recruitment of 250 *volontaires* (volunteer) chaplains. De Mun established an office in the headquarters of the Croix Rouge (Red Cross) and recruited men through *L'Écho de Paris*. He was quickly inundated with volunteers and with donations to support the initial costs of the volunteers. By November 12, 1914, Minister of War Alexandre Millerand issued a circular supporting a daily indemnity of ten francs and a double ration for the volunteers who had the rights of the grade of lieutenant.[29]

The Bureau of Volunteer Chaplains, as it was called, received applicants not only from priests in France but also from those in missionary outposts. Applicants had to be free of military obligations, have their bishop's authorization, and enjoy good health. Each applicant was given a personal interview.[30]

Assignments were coordinated with the army's Health Service because all chaplains were assigned through that service. Two men were recruited to assist with the volume of applicants and the organization. These were Geoffroy de Grandmaison, a collaborator of De Mun's in his efforts in Social Catholicism, and François Veuillot, a journalist associated with *L'Univers*, the conservative Catholic publication led most famously in the nineteenth century by his uncle, Louis Veuillot.

Given the mass troop movements and confusion of the early days of the war, there were many problems with initiating the service of chaplains. Because the government offices had moved to Bordeaux and De Mun with them, Grandmaison was left in charge. Communications with the front were difficult. In one instance, Grandmaison went from place to place with a group of five chaplains, who could not find their assignments. Many others suffered the same problems because it was difficult to find where priests were needed. The Bureau was receiving complaints about the lack of chaplains, but they were powerless to assign chaplains without knowing where they were needed.[31]

In his notes and impressions on the war published in 1920, Abbé Lelièvre recounts his confusion after he had been accepted as a volunteer chaplain. On August 25 he wrote: "No news of this affair of the chaplaincy. One is busy, however, since they warned us that we leave without pay and that we double the official chaplains. What does that mean? Will there be two, where there was one? Or how many newcomers will be understudies? Doubling without pay an official chaplain with a copious salary, . . . the volunteer chaplain will not have a very level road under his feet, and I imagine that he will have to endure abnegation; to his colleague also."

Despite this confusion, Lelièvre recounted, Grandmaison told the volunteers that "it is important to leave." Lelièvre agreed, asserting: "The rest will arrange itself. In fact, there was no plan to have us [volunteer chaplains] in the war. We will figure it out . . . like the war. It is already very beautiful, it seems, that the government accepts our black cassocks on the battlefield. It is bound by the law, the regulations, the administration, the Chamber of Deputies. . . . Let us be grateful to the government in principle. For me, I prefer this. Volunteer chaplain, without pay, that will be the dream . . . after the war. And perhaps during."[32]

By August 27, the Red Cross intervened and finally sent Lelièvre to the Gare de Laon in the region of Picardy, where he was to await orders for an assignment to a "sanitary formation." But when he and other priests arrived, no one knew where to send them because they were not expected. Although they were greeted sympathetically, they had to go from one unit commander to another in the direction of Étaples, and finally to the headquarters of the Health Service. Then, thanks to a Colonel de Laborie, they were authorized to take the first train, which passed to a hospital near the front.[33]

Further complicating matters, other priests sought appointments to the chaplaincy on their own initiative when neither the Bureau of Volunteer Chaplains nor the Health Service responded to their requests. One of these, Abbé Achille Liénart, was not subject to mobilization when the war began because he had completed his military duty and had been discharged in 1907. After an education that included higher degrees from the Sorbonne and biblical studies at the Institut Catholique in Paris and in Rome, he had served as professor of Holy Scripture at the diocesan seminary at Cambrai in 1910. He was on vacation when the war broke, but he felt he could not stay behind.

He had earlier given his name to the archbishop of Cambrai, who had anticipated the need for chaplains should war break out. But he found no official chaplaincy available when he applied to the Health Service. After some days of searching, his cousin advised him to approach the head doctor of a medical-surgical unit that was being formed in Lille. The doctor signed a letter, which Liénart himself composed on August 9, authorizing him to accompany the 3d ambulance of the 51st reserve division. He wrote: "It was understood furthermore, between me and the head doctor, that I asked for nothing, neither payment, nor food, nor provision of any sort, especially not a place among the officers, but only permission to accompany the nurses to provide aid to the wounded. All the rest was abandoned to the care of God!" He described his reception: "A little astonished by the presence of this priest in a cassock, with a large hat and carrying a sack on his back, the nurses and the soldiers in charge greeted me cordially nonetheless, for in this grave hour a great wind of union sacrée was sweeping the country."[34]

Once at the front, the various conflicts and ambiguities inherent in the priests' situation became even more apparent. Disorganization plagued the chaplaincy throughout the war, forcing priests into circumstances in which they had both the opportunity and the challenge of finding ways to fulfill their assignments, whether military or religious. Priests enjoyed more autonomy than they ordinarily had, which worried both the Church and the military hierarchy.

The first internal Church reports, written by two priests, were dated 1915, after the first year of war. Georges Ardant, director of education and charitable works in the diocese of Limoges, was himself a volunteer chaplain with the 29th Infantry Division. His report outlined a number of problems. First, he stated that it was "shocking" to see the chaplains named by a layman when ecclesiastical authority would know better how to recruit them. This was true not only of the volunteers but also of the official chaplains who were chosen by the Ministry of War. Secondly, he indicated that some of the chaplains were more concerned with glory than with the supernatural and the well-being of souls. Some vainly played the soldier and took on the habits of the officers, smoking and drinking in cafés.

Ardant's primary concern, however, was with the disorganization, stemming, he believed, from the lack of hierarchical authority. He stated that because chaplains were stationed with the stretcher-bearers of the corps, they had little to do. A head chaplain, chosen by ecclesiastical authority, could divide the tasks and provide for the best use of the priests in his unit. He asserted that it was "urgent to better distribute the work."[35]

The second report, dated October 15, 1915, was authored by Abbé Couget, a volunteer chaplain with the 39th infantry brigade; it focused specifically on the organization of the military chaplaincy in France. Couget explained that his conversations and correspondence with military chaplains had uncovered a series of problems. Like Ardant, he blamed the unequal distribution of chaplains on the absence of an overall hierarchical authority. He also claimed that some chaplains favored certain troops and neglected others. In some instances, women in the various regions were better served than the troops. He recommended a definition of territory in which chaplains would be under an ecclesiastical superior.

Secondly, he also agreed with Ardant that laymen were not qualified to estimate the merits of an ecclesiastical candidate. Only bishops could and should determine which priests should serve as chaplains. The Bureau of Volunteer Chaplains had to be led back to its true role of presenting to the military authority candidates selected by ecclesiastical authority.

Finally, he complained that soldier priests, combatants and noncombatants, performed ministerial functions in an independent fashion. He believed they had to be controlled by the chaplains. But to enforce this, an ecclesiastical authority must regulate the canonical relationship between the chaplains and the soldier priests. He recommended that the pope appoint a Grand Aumônier des armées (chaplain-in-chief for all the army). He suggested specifically that the pope should renew the tradition of having the archbishop of Paris serve in that role. He, in turn, would choose two *coadjuteurs* (assistant bishops) from among the military chaplains to manage the activities.[36]

Bearing out these reports, some of the volunteer chaplains complained about overbearing titulaire chaplains. In one such complaint to the Bureau of Volunteer Chaplains, Abbé Charles-Léon Flaus claimed that an official chaplain immobilized the volunteer chaplains by insisting that nothing be done without his approval.[37] Abbé Lelièvre also charged that one official chaplain would not give the stretcher-bearer priests permission to say mass, and refused to allow the volunteer chaplains to serve with the regiments.[38]

The problem of hierarchical control could never be solved, according to the historian Xavier Boniface, because the appointment of a chaplain-in-chief collided with the separation of church and state. The situation was made worse by the absence of diplomatic relations between France and the Holy See. Pope Benedict XV proposed as a compromise that two chaplains who were bishops be appointed as ecclesiastical inspectors. On November 19, 1917, the Consistorial Congregation of the Vatican named Bishop Charles Ruch and Bishop Gabriel de Llobet "ecclesiastical inspectors of the armies," with the power to visit and direct all the priests in the army. Military authorities neither confirmed the assignment nor provided the material means for Ruch and Llobet to exercise their powers. For their part, the bishops did not embrace the arrangement for fear of diminishing their own authority over their priests. The result was that the official chaplains were left free to organize themselves and the volunteer chaplains and the priest soldiers they could recruit to help them.[39]

Issues of hierarchical control were also compounded by the fact that the priests were all subject to military authority. The Ministry of War controlled the assignments of the titulaire chaplains, while De Mun's Bureau of Volunteer Chaplains selected the volontaires chaplains who served under the authority of the Health Service. In the field, the head doctors assigned the volunteer chaplains as they saw fit. Then there was a third kind of chaplain, the *bénévole*, or unofficial volunteer, who had a military assignment as a combatant, stretcher-bearer, or nurse, and was thus subject to a military commander. Both titulaires and volontaires were expected to serve at aid stations miles from the front. Most priests felt they were most needed at the front and often convinced their commanders to assign them to one regiment or battalion. But neither the Ministry of War nor the Health Service approved of such assignments.

Soldier priests and priest officers, on the other hand, were uniquely positioned to provide the comforts and rites of religion in the trenches and at the front, but only with the permission of their commanding officers. In some cases, they were recruited by the titulaires, in others, military commanders sought their help, and in still others they acted on their own initiative. Some commanders, even those who were not Catholic, saw the benefits of the priests' services and despite the disapproval of the War Office, assigned them to work as chaplains exclusively. When the military learned that this was happening, the Ministry issued an order on June 26, 1916, requiring that any soldier priest had to complete regular military duties before engaging in any religious activities.[40]

Military authorities were not concerned with the equitable distribution of the many priests in the army. Grandmaison and Veuillot cited an article of P. Décout's in *Revue du clergé français*, which claimed that the chaplaincy suffered from three evils: inadequate numbers, poor distribution, and unfortunate administrative assignments. A letter from the Jesuit chaplain Georges Guitton dated February 17, 1916, blamed the problem on the government's conviction that the priest was only good for burying a person or perhaps to console him at the last moment of life. There was no apparent appreciation for the priests' role among the living, he claimed. "The fundamental mistake," he believed, was the conscription law itself, which he described as "unjust . . . anti-French and anti-military, which, under pretext of equality, has mobilized as soldiers of the second class valuable priests who should have had a place in the Chaplaincy."[41]

Complaints about the maldistribution flowed into the offices of the Bureau of Volunteer Chaplains. Abbé Louis Brochard wrote in the middle of the fighting in September 1914 that there were four chaplains in a formation of stretcher-bearers, which included already fifty priests, while Abbé Sainte-Marie complained "that certain official chaplains, imprisoned so to speak in groups of stretcher bearers in a Corps . . . are somewhat considered to be in a cushy assignment, away from the front lines."[42] Abbé Marie-Jacques Casteljau's letter of November 29, 1915, described a typical outcome: "We are three official chaplains in the same encampment, far from our troops, which are dispersed in many communes. The soldiers are busy all day. And when at six in the evening they are free, how can we go to them when we are 6, 8, 10, 15, or 25 kilometers distant from them and night is falling, or it is raining, or freezing, or there is no cover where they are."[43]

Despite their openly generous approval of priests' mobilization, bishops and religious superiors worried about the spiritual as well as the physical well-being of these men. First, they focused on clearly defining the duties and privileges of priests in conditions of war. Canon law prohibited a member of the clergy from active engagement in combat. Since they were forced into these positions by the laws of France, the bishops solicited advice from the Vatican as early as 1912 when threats of war began to loom during the Moroccan crisis. A letter from the secretary of state of the Vatican, dated November 22, 1914, reconfirmed the edict of the Sacred Penitentiary in 1912. The edict provided a special dispensation for priests called up by their government into military service. They were allowed to celebrate mass and administer the sacraments—that is to say, they lost none of their priestly prerogatives. They had the authorization of the Holy See to be a part of the combatant army. After the war priests were to submit themselves to a competent authority to be exonerated.[44]

During the war, the Vatican dispensed mobilized clergy from reciting the prayers in their breviary except when at rest. In November 1914 the Vatican exempted the wounded from fasting before receiving the Eucharist. The exemption was extended to all soldiers at the front in February 1915. Rome also provided that soldiers could make their confessions to any priest, even if the priest was not serving as a chaplain. Also in February of 1915, the Vatican granted permission for group absolution of troops. If there was not time for confession, any priest could prepare a group of soldiers to receive absolution. Rome also loosened the rules concerning the hours that mass could be celebrated. It was very soon clear that it was impossible to follow the rules that limited the celebration from an hour before dawn to an hour after noon. Also priests were allowed to celebrate mass in the presence of heretics and the excommunicated.[45]

The pope himself worried about the spiritual well-being of the priests at war. *Le Prêtre aux Armées* on March 15, 1916, described a letter sent by Pope Benedict XV to Mgr. François-Léon Gauthey, archbishop of Besançon, which expressed concern for the morality of soldier priests, especially when at rest, and offered them advice on remaining faithful and being an example.

In a number of ways, bishops and religious superiors worked to sustain their soldier priests' morale through communication as well as retreats and special workshops. They tried to make sure that they did not lose contact with their priests during the war. Many letters, accumulated in archives and books and published in Catholic national and diocesan papers, document their frequent communication. Priests were very conscientious about writing to their superiors to describe conditions at the front, to reassure them of their spiritual well-being, to ask for assistance, and to express gratitude. For example, there are many letters in the archival files of the archbishop of Rouen, Cardinal Louis-Ernest Dubois, that thank him for the woolen sweaters and other amenities he had sent to the front.[46] Bishops also required priests to attend days of prayer and reflection, if they were stationed near the headquarters of their dioceses.

Official chaplains also attempted to provide for the spiritual sustenance of other priests in the military. They tried to gather the priests in their units for prayers and camaraderie whenever possible. Grandmaison and Veuillot described the actions of one chaplain, Abbé Adrien Pangaud, who, upon arriving at the 27th division at the end of 1915, called together the bénévoles and offered his services to them. He established a meeting every Sunday where they could come and get what they needed: hosts, rosaries, manuals, and vestments. He planned to visit each of them and their troops. Abbé Flaus, chaplain of the 39th Corps, in turn provided the thirty stretcher-bearer priests in his unit "a weekly spiritual meeting and also a meal where, each week, they have the enjoyment of finding themselves fraternally reunited." Abbé Jean-Marie Desgranges announced a reunion of forty priests of his group and of his ambulance. Others recounted similar meetings. Abbé Auguste Limagne wrote on January 15, 1916: "I strove, particularly . . . to develop relationships with all the priests of the division, to organize their priestly activity a little, to fortify their interior life by facilitating their celebration of mass, by furnishing what they would lack for worship."[47]

Le Prêtre aux Armées, a bulletin launched in February 1915, circulated among the priests at the front, chaplains, nurses, stretcher-bearers, and regular soldiers. The first issue stated that it was established "to remedy in some manner the intellectual and moral privations of the clergy in the armies," isolated from "priestly society." Each issue offered advice, reports, meditations and spiritual readings, a summary of official military communiqués, and letters from readers.[48]

The archdiocese of Paris began its own newsletter, *Le Clergé de Paris aux Armées*, in 1915 as well. The archdiocese proposed to give the priests news of their "priestly family." The first issue, dated July 1, 1915, stated that the archdiocese had more than four hundred priests mobilized, including just forty-two chaplains, either official or volunteer. Their names and assignments were listed so that their colleagues could seek them out. This issue quoted Cardinal Amette's letter of January 1, 1915, to his priests and seminarians "under the flag": "During all these sad weeks, your Archbishop, gentlemen, has not ceased to follow you in his thoughts, in his heart, and in his prayers."[49] In the second issue, dated August 1915, there is also a letter from the archbishop urging the mobilized priests to virtue and piety at the front. A short article praises Abbé Auguste Le Bouteiller, an adjutant who was killed in battle, for never forgetting his duty as a priest even while performing his duties as a sub-officer.[50]

Superiors of religious orders also sent out monthly bulletins to their members at the front. The Franciscan *État militaire* published news of the monks who had become soldiers as well as the letters they sent to the provincial, and listed their promotions, wounds, and citations. Other members of the order found encouragement and pride in this news as well as a connection to their brothers. The fifty-four-year-old Franciscan Édouard de Massat, who had returned from missionary work in Canada to volunteer as a chaplain, wrote to his provincial after receiving one of these bulletins at the end of April 1915: "With what pleasure I read the very edifying and comforting letters of my brothers. All exude devotion, self-sacrifice, and love for France. All are vibrant with a seraphic spirit. One feels it pulsing across the surface of the words. Also never have I felt so proud of the brothers and of my Order."[51]

The Sulpicians published a bulletin for their seminarians and at the end of the war published excerpts from letters of one hundred seminarians who had been killed at the front. The letters had been written to their spiritual directors and members of their families. The editor asserted that the letters demonstrated that the seminarians were rooted in pious exercises, which helped them retain their spiritual life even amidst the material conditions of the war. The easiest and simplest exercise, he claimed, was the rosary: "Often, under the leadership of a seminarian, a little group of combatants repeats with fervor the series of Ave Marias."[52]

The Bureau of Volunteer Chaplains and the Catholic press helped organize volunteers to provide priests with money, portable altars, medals, books, and small gifts they could distribute among the troops, including sweaters, socks, and other items of clothing. This help was especially vital for the bénévoles, who had neither pay nor official status. Abbé Pierre-Louis Hachin of the 162nd Infantry wrote on September 20, 1915, to thank the Bureau on behalf of his soldiers for the one hundred francs he received each month: "They are numerous, indeed, here, the brave soldiers from the invaded territories who have not found a *marraine* (a wartime godmother), have only their daily penny to get themselves a treat; a cigarette, a bar of chocolate, a newspaper are opportunities to do them a good turn." Another priest, Abbé Emmanuel Danigo, wrote on May 16, 1916: "Your generosity permits me to relieve many miseries, to approach some men up until now hostile to priests, to exercise, in a word, a fruitful apostolate."[53]

With these donations, ambitious chaplains established reading rooms. Abbé André David of the 6th Colonial explained in a letter to the Bureau that the soldiers have "a very great desire to read, because they are bored in their trenches." He congratulated himself for having been able to set up reading rooms thanks to the Société de Secours aux Blessés Militaires and to the Société Bibliographique. Abbé Louis Fillon wrote that his library had 1,200 volumes and 1,000 were in circulation.[54] Others built chapels in their dugouts where soldiers could come to pray and hear mass.

The history of long years of anticlerical sentiment and clerical sensitivity did not totally disappear with the union sacrée. Hints of the consciousness of the past were manifest in comments like the following from Abbé Bourceret. He wrote that he fraternized with everyone on the train to their gathering point at Fontainebleau, and commented: "The cassock does not terrify any more; they are not afraid of it, they seek it out. It seems that it has become a talisman for those who are leaving and that it will protect from divine anger."[55] Later, however, he overheard the doctors talking jovially with each other while smoking their pipes. One of them, whom he described as "dominant," swore liberally and declared himself anticlerical. Nonetheless, Bourceret made a joke of it, commenting: "I imagine, however, that there will not be any 'eating of the three priests' in his medical unit. To eat a curé is dangerous and so difficult to digest."[56]

Even the praise for the chaplains recounted by Grandmaison and Veuillot demonstrates these latent attitudes. They were particularly careful to point out praise from officers and men who were not practicing Catholics. In one instance they quoted an adjutant, who affirmed one day after returning from battle: "I am not a buddy of curés. My testimony is not therefore suspect. Well, believe me, friends, without the curés, many wounded would have died on the battlefield without being noticed."[57] And there seems to be a defensive strategy in the care with which *La Croix* included a special column, in each issue during the war, listing the military citations priests received that confirmed both their bravery and their solicitude for the men.[58]

Voices within the press as well as within the military itself expressed suspicion with regard to the activities of the priests on the battlefield, at the aid stations, and in the hospitals. As early as October 1914, *La Croix* cited the response of the *Semaine Catholique de Toulouse* to accusations that clergy pressured the wounded men to fulfill their religious duties. *La Croix* asserted in their defense: "No pressure . . . from anywhere. It is in full liberty that one comes or one abstains! But how few abstain!"[59] Forty-one-year-old Abbé Léonce Raffin, who left his parish of St. Louis d'Antin in Paris to serve first as a stretcher-bearer and later as a volunteer chaplain, wrote in his memoir that in December 1917 commanders were warned: "It remains understood that acts of proselytism are rigorously forbidden and that chaplains of the armies are bound by all the rules and obligations of military discipline."[60]

There was a huge uproar in the press over the sermon of Abbé Jean Lagardère of Besançon, the fifty-four-year-old chaplain of the 8th Division of the cavalry. Lagardère, who had a peasant background, had earned a doctor-ate in canon law and theology from the French seminary in Rome. Before the war, he had worked in the diocese of Besançon as director of diocesan charitable works and was a renowned preacher, not only in France but also across Europe. When the war began, he and his colleague Abbé Joseph-Eugène Payen, eager to be of service, applied and were accepted as official chaplains by the Ministry of War. On October 6, 1915, as the 18th Dragoons prepared to attack, he said mass in the woods for the regiment. In his sermon he claimed that France was expiating for national faults and errors by the blood shed in the war. He stated: "France, staggering under the weight of its errors and national mistakes, had need to make itself worthy of conquering, of a bloody purification." When his sermon ended, the eight hundred cavalry men present fell on their knees, some with tears in their eyes, and the chaplain recited the formula of general absolution as he had promised.[61]

When they returned from the battlefield at Champagne, Lagardère found that he had been attacked in several newspapers, including the *Petit Parisien* and *Le Temps*, for sectarianism, for daring to talk of national crimes and the need for expiation. They called upon Minister of War Joseph Galliéni to dismiss him. Although Catholic newspapers defended him, Galliéni decided to order an investigation by the General Staff. Ultimately Lagardère was suspended for fifteen days for having "pronounced in front of the troops . . . some inappropriate words that offend public feeling."[62] He did not comment on the punishment as a soldier, he asserted, but as a priest he protested that the sentence seemed unjustified. He claimed that the soldiers who heard him were inspired to give their lives for France. He said: "I challenge you to find one person who supports your condemnation. I have strengthened their souls, I have intensified their patriotism; I have been a good soldier and a good priest." And, indeed, Lagardère reputedly continued this theme in his sermons without losing the love and respect of the soldiers and without any further disciplinary action.[63]

Some priests were criticized for over-identifying with the military. It became enough of an issue that the Ministry of War issued an official complaint in 1917. Léonce Raffin, serving as a volunteer chaplain in Lorraine in 1917, described the problem: "Certain chaplains, haunted by the prestige of the officers, wear their cap and their sleeves [with stripes] over their cassocks and on their overcoats. They have forgotten that if they have the salary of a captain, they do not have the grade in the military hierarchy." He stated that one day the head doctor, who wore five stripes, asked him to tell one of his chaplain colleagues to stop wearing the insignia of an officer. He said he fulfilled the commission very delicately but was rather coolly received by the excellent chaplain, who was very courageous and proud of serving his battalion of cavalry. He commented derisively: "To cover his sacerdotal ministry with the prestige of an officer, what an aberration! And, in my thoughts, I called to mind the chaplain [Édouard] Turgis, my contemporary, holy priest, free of all vanity, who found the dead on the Somme."[64]

Abbé Couget's 1915 report had also mentioned this problem as a cause of resentment among officers. He explained that a highly placed member of the military asserted that some of the young priests "fitted themselves as officers . . . and seemed to want to appear more officer than priest—what was intended in providing military chaplains was to have *priests*, and neither officers, nor soldiers." Couget said that this remark was made by a person who was known to be rather favorable to clergy and recognized "the moral benefit" that the priest can have in the army."[65]

The Third Republic's novel policy of drafting priests to serve in the war, much against tradition and expectations, went forward, replete with problems of organization, discipline, and misunderstandings. These were exacerbated by the fact that diplomatic relations between the Vatican and France had been severed, along with official communication between the government and the Church hierarchy, with the Separation Law of 1905. The two institutions most noted for hierarchical structures and discipline, the Church and the military, were confronted with a situation in which these strictures on communication made the ordinary processes of discipline nearly impossible.

Government officials, the military commanders, bishops, religious superiors, and the priests themselves were left to establish new relationships in the very difficult circumstances of the battlefield. Because of the Third Republic's attitude toward religion, priests, even those serving as chaplains, were disbursed according to military concerns rather than religious. But because the priest was still a priest, even if a combat soldier, military commanders frequently bent the rules to allow him to serve the religious needs of the troops.

Ecclesiastical discipline, which had always been the guiding force in the lives of priests, was exceptionally confused. The chaplain, official or volunteer, was directly responsible to a military authority rather than to any distant ecclesiastical superior. In turn, his authority over soldier priests, who were nurses, stretcher-bearers, or combatants, was unclear and could be overturned by military authority. Although religious superiors and bishops maintained contact with priests on the battlefield and sought to provide support, communication was infrequent, subject to the exigencies of war. Thus priests were experiencing an autonomy and a flexibility they had never known. Each individual had to figure out his own path for reconciling himself to the reality of war and at the same time fulfilling his own expectations and hopes for being both a good priest and a good soldier. In their own words of hope and struggle, the following chapters recount the odyssey that brought them closer to their countrymen and to a new understanding of the meaning of their priesthood and their citizenship.

CHAPTER THREE

PRIESTS AS MISSIONARIES ON THE BATTLEFIELDS

Afver years of separation from the men of France, more than 32,000 French priests and religious took their places among three-quarters of the male population of France—eight million men throughout the course of the war.[1]

As he went off to war, the priest faced an incredible challenge. Not only did he have to deal with the horrors of war and its moral dilemmas but also with his very real fears about acceptance or rejection by fellow soldiers. After years of anticlerical legislation and increasing isolation from the French populace, priests were acutely sensitive to signs of animosity. At the same time, they were extremely hopeful that they would have a new opportunity to influence men who had fallen away from religious observance or who had never been exposed to it. At some level, each of them seemed to regard this opportunity as the mitigating factor to the otherwise compromising situation of a priest at war.

Even combatants were preoccupied with the religious mission. In fact, they seemed anxious to confirm that they had a unique opportunity to influence their fellow soldiers. The youngest of the soldier priests expressed the most concern about being accepted by their fellow soldiers and about how to avail themselves of the opportunities to influence them. At the same time, they were worried that they would be corrupted by the immoral or crude behavior of the barracks and the trenches. Older priests, who had accepted commissions as officers during their previous military training, were much more sanguine about their ability to combine their military and priestly obligations.

Stretcher-bearers and nurses also sought to be accepted and longed for opportunities to offer religious services to the men. Chaplains, of course, focused on their religious mission, but their impact and influence was often impeded by the exigencies of the battlefield as well as their inadequate distribution. They often felt the need to work for acceptance by the men, and were wary of manifestations of anticlericalism.

This chapter describes the priests' ever-present concern to be missionaries on the battlefield. In the early days of the war, they were almost giddy over the new opportunities to serve the many soldiers who seemed to have found a new interest in religion. As the war wore on, however, even the most successful chaplains experienced times of bitter disillusionment. Nonetheless, their persistence in the face of many obstacles brought them a nuanced understanding of their complex relationship with their fellow soldiers and of their priestly mission.

A letter from Abbé Louis Castelin to *La Croix*, written on September 18, 1914, clearly reflects the enthusiasm priests felt in the heady days of religious revival at the beginning of the war. From his vantage point as chaplain of the 29th Division of the 15th Corps, he wrote: "In the midst of these sorrows and horrors, there are some reasons to thank God. The war is a great mission, and it is God who is in charge of preaching, leaving to his priests and in particular to his military chaplains the task of gathering in the fruits."[2]

Young seminarians expressed the most concern over fitting in to the military and, at the same time, an almost naive hope to have influence over men who had not been practicing religion. Despite their worries about being accepted by the men, they feared being contaminated by exposure to bad morals and to the demands of war. Letters to family members and religious superiors detailed both the soldiers' reactions to their presence and the most effective methods for withstanding corrupting influences. They seemed to be trying as much to convince themselves as to reassure their families and superiors that everything was going to be fine.

Bernard Lavergne's letter to his cousin from the barracks in Rouen on October 23, 1913, asserted that she was right to believe that he could have influence over the other soldiers: "You cannot imagine—but yes, it is you who told me so on Sunday—how much good one can accomplish with the soldiers. This daily contact with the men places us in a position to know them very well. Moreover, they are often simple and trusting, especially in the regiments." He believed that "a discreet apostolate" would be the most effective to lead men back to the faith. He had great confidence in his beliefs and thought his best preaching would be the silent, simple example of his faith.[3]

The twenty-three-year-old Lavergne was the thirteenth of fifteen children born to a stained-glass artist. His entire education had been in the seminary, both minor and major seminaries, in the diocese of Versailles. He was called up for duty in 1913 prior to taking his ordination to the priesthood. Dispatched in early 1915 to the front near Arras and promoted to corporal, he wrote to his mother on March 18 that he could have even more influence now that he had command over twelve men.[4]

Lavergne's concerns and enthusiasm were echoed in the correspondence of Jean Nourisson, who was mobilized in August 1914 at twenty-one years of age, after a year's deferment because he was in the Saint Sulpice seminary at Issy. Soon after he arrived at the front, he was made an officer cadet who would lead men in combat. He was pleasantly surprised by his reception in the barracks and believed he was having a good influence on the men. He wrote to a young seminarian friend on August 19, 1914: "I have told you already, I believe, that I have been very well received as a seminarian. . . . Very many tell me about their little concerns. The good Christians thank me for being there to remind them of their curé and their Church by my presence. The half-indifferent speak to me willingly of their broad-minded spirit, sometimes of the way in which they lost their faith."[5]

In those first days of the war, he predicted a solid renewal of piety: "You say yourself, the spectacle is very heart-warming: everywhere there is a renewal of piety and of solid religion. The war will be horrific and will make many weep, but it will perhaps signal a renewal in our country."[6] He understood that his influence would be slow, writing later in the month on August 26:

I find very much sympathy. They [the soldiers] watch conversations in front of me and I have already had some opportunities to explain my ideas. I have been attacked only once, and by a person of such bad faith that I have informed him that I would not discuss anything more with him. Some question me willingly about my 'metier,' and, without seeming to, I am able to break down some prejudices against priests. . . . I am happy to be in their opinion a very good boy, speaking willingly with them when the occasion arises. . . . I would have been thrilled if in my footsteps, the converts would flock around me, that the blind would see, etc. . . . I will have a slower and more obscure ministry, even in my eyes. . . . I have to resign myself to it, but it also is hard.[7]

Nourrisson was also concerned to confirm the strength of his commitment to his vocation and to religious discipline, as much to reassure himself as his friends and superiors. Writing to a younger seminarian who would soon be mobilized, he explained that he believed that his spiritual well-being would be enhanced by life in the military: "When I have more experience of the life of the regiment, I will be able to give you more useful advice and practical details. I am convinced from now on a delicate conscience can only gain in strength in the regiment, without being shaken, if it takes the required precautions." He warned: "Pray now for all these intentions, you will never do it too soon."[8]

Marcel Baillat's correspondence also reflected that same mixture of trepidation about mingling with other soldiers and hope that he might evangelize them, typical of the young seminarian. An eighteen-year-old seminarian at Nantes, Baillat had enlisted in the military before he would have been eligible for the draft. In fact, he would have been excused from military service because he had had polio in his younger years. The son of a widow of a colonial administrator, he had been raised in Paris. When his mother died in 1912 he decided to become a priest. When the war broke out he was convinced his country needed him, so he begged for permission to volunteer for military duty. Once in the trenches, however, he fluctuated between feeling isolated among fellows who did not understand his yearning to be a priest, and believing he was having an influence on his comrades. In a letter on March 3, 1915, he wrote: "I am 'the baby' of the company, the others are the 'grandfathers.' A 'baby' is allowed everything, even persistence with the old 'foxes' who have long ago given up their religious duties."[9]

When he returned from England to join the military at the beginning of the war, the Jesuit novice René de la Perraudière was just twenty-two years old. He was quickly promoted, first to corporal, then to sergeant in January 1915. He was from a noble family and constantly criticized himself for not embracing his apostolic responsibilities more enthusiastically. In a letter to his novice director, he wrote:

I find myself full of desires for an apostolate, but rather awkward in realizing them, and rather lax in overcoming this awkwardness. I feel like a stranger to everyone, mistrusted by several, because I am a 'curé.' At least I believe they feel that way (I am too preoccupied with what they think of me), and that is difficult to bear. . . . Please God that I can at least give an example of the spirit of duty. . . . Can the desire to change a situation improve it? Perhaps: but it seems to me that in a more elevated social milieu, in the milieu of the officer, I would do more good.[10]

Xavier Thérésette, a twenty-four-year-old Franciscan seminarian, the second of seven children from a devout working-class family from Reims, had returned from Belgium for his military training. Even though he had completed his years of service by the time the war began, he had returned to defend his country. He seemed certain at the end of 1914 that war would result in a re-Christianization of France. Soon after being promoted to second lieutenant, he wrote to his provincial from the front at Verdun:

What I hope for is that it would be a year of grandeur and renewal for our France; you will see this triumph, beloved Father, you will taste it and you will have the joy of seeing again the France of years past, that is to say, the true Christian France. May the good Virgin bless these wishes, who watches over her poor children and if the good Master permits it, may we all obtain the grace of seeing each other again after this long and terrible war is finished.[11]

Older priest combatants, who had accepted commissions in the military reserve when they completed their required military service, did not share the younger seminarians' uncertainty about their reception by the troops. They also looked forward to the opportunity to exercise their apostolic responsibilities. Their very emphasis on their dual role seems to demonstrate that they felt a need to justify their presence on the battlefield. One of these, Pierre Durouchoux, a forty-year-old Jesuit, was from a military family of bourgeois Parisian origin. He was the last of nine children. His grandfather had died fighting the Communards in 1870 and his father was decorated in the same battle with the Legion of Honor. Durouchoux was not conflicted at all, but rather was confident that he was able to combine his position as captain with his role as priest. He was convinced that his rank supported his priestly authority. On June 1, 1915, he wrote a friend: "You know that I am largely able to exercise my ministry, and that mitigates the experience, and gives my present existence a second very dear reason. I double as an officer and a chaplain; and the stripes facilitate my apostolic action. . . . God be praised that I am employed amongst these souls. There were very many who made their Easter Duty, and the 'returns' continue."[12]

In witness to both Durouchoux's battle readiness and his effectiveness as a priest, a Catholic lieutenant, Paul Tézenas du Montcel, wrote in his journal of a surprise meeting with him near Reims in January 1915. He said "a tall, solid, well built, bearded officer, with a small pipe in his mouth introduced himself as Sergeant Durouchoux. This is the Jesuit father people told me about yesterday and it is the first time that I have seen a Jesuit built like this!" In March Tézenas found Durouchoux, now a second lieutenant, saying mass, and remarked on his "simple and moving" sermon.[13]

Jean Julien Weber embraced a role in the military as an officer. He came from a military family and a pious one. His upbringing in Strasbourg made him a staunch patriot. Drawn toward the priesthood as well, he entered Saint Sulpice Seminary in October 1905 and took up required military service in 1908, serving two years. He was given the right to become a reserve officer on October 1, 1910, with the rank of corporal. He justified his choice in his later memoir stating that he firmly believed that being an officer gave him a better opportunity for apostolic effectiveness. He said that as a simple soldier he would feel "paralyzed," while as an officer he would be better able to "make my faith manifest."[14]

Promoted to sergeant and then to second lieutenant in the reserve, he wrote that his military service brought him in contact "with the moral poverty of so many of my comrades, peasants or workers at the Japy or Peugeot factories. This contact has shown me evidence that there are not only intellectual problems but also problems of the soul." He believed that through this experience he was cured of his "exaggerated intellectualism."[15]

Indeed, Weber declared that he was prepared to be a "new kind of apostle." Again reflecting in his memoir years later, he articulated his hopes as he went to war. He felt prepared by his classical and spiritual training and his theological and biblical research to sustain discussions with nonbelievers. His two years of active military service, he believed, prepared him for his military responsibilities. He wrote: "I was able, then, without temerity, to hope that this new existence in the war would find me not only faithful, but capable of being a new kind of apostle. . . . I was able to hope not only to live through the war, but to grow in experience for my future work. The sense of responsibilities increased my Christian feeling, so that I returned to my normal life better equipped to do the work of God. . . . The service of the country must have also prepared me for my service as priest."[16]

His descriptions of battles reflect the concerns of an officer; nonetheless he recounts giving absolution to men on the battlefield, rejoicing in his freedom to be in the midst of the action. He believed that as an officer he had a distinct advantage over chaplains. He explained: "In the line, the officer priest enjoys a certain mobility which permits him to travel not only in the trenches . . . but even to the front lines. One can approach the wounded, give them absolution, anoint the dying, which a military chaplain, tied to his aide post or facing the impossibility of crossing the lines of fire, is not able to do."[17]

Those priests and seminarians who were inducted into the service prior to 1905 had been promised that in time of war they could choose to serve in a noncombat position, which better suited the canonical prohibition against killing. Assigned to take care of the wounded or rescue them from the battle-field, these men were subject to the orders of their superiors and were not free to perform priestly duties as much as they would have liked. Nonetheless they were enthusiastic at the beginning of the war about their new opportunities.

One of the most famous of these was the Jesuit Pierre Teilhard de Chardin, who later gained a worldwide reputation as a paleontologist and philosopher. Born in 1881 to an aristocratic family from the region of Clermont-Ferrand, he had been called up to serve in the military at age nineteen but was deferred because he was in the novitiate. His "class" of 1901 was still one in which he was allowed to choose noncombat duty if mobilized in time of war. He chose to be a stretcher-bearer and served with the 8th Regiment of Moroccan riflemen, which also included Zouaves (a regiment of assault troops). He provided a thoughtful and almost brutally honest account of his experiences as a stretcher-bearer throughout the entire war, on battlefields in Belgium, Picardy, and Verdun, in letters to his cousin, Marguerite Teillard-Chambon. He saw the war as "a chance to act as a person in his relation with men whose life he was sharing."[18] He stated: "For us soldier-priests, war was a baptism into reality."[19]

In his early letters he was enthusiastic in his conviction that he had a great opportunity to influence the religious convictions of the men. From Marest in the Oise he wrote on February 9, 1915: "I feel increasingly happy at having been posted to a regiment in which, as I told you, I am the only priest, and where there is a large number of men who, when the time comes, will turn to me for help. I hope really to have found my right place."[20] A few days later in a letter dated February 24–25, 1915, he described his activities and his hopes for influence:

> [F]rom my point of view, what is really interesting has been to find that in my cellar and its vicinity the men were very approachable. I haven't, of course, made any conversions, nor given anyone absolution (the dangers we encounter are, at the moment, too trifling: not one man has been wounded during the past ten days); but I have made contact with many fine lads. . . . On Sunday I said mass in the colonel's cellar, and dined with one of the officers:—on Monday I shared the machine-gun sergeant-major's stew; and so on. . . . All this, I hope, will gradually establish me as the priest-comrade to whom a man can turn when things go wrong. Pray hard that this may come about.[21]

In the opening days of the war, Abbé J. M. Bourceret volunteered to serve as a sergeant-nurse at the age of forty-four. Before the war, he had been a professor at Notre Dame des Champs, Paris, and a vicar at the Cathedral of Saint Ouen in Rouen. He had already served his military duty in 1891 and had been discharged. Bourceret was surprised and pleased by the favorable greetings he received as he crossed Paris on his bicycle with the flag of the Red Cross. The sense of relief and even vindication implied in his comments reflects his experiences during the period of the separation of church and state. The school in Paris at which he was a professor was forced to move to Fontenay aux Roses, a commune southwest of the city.

He observed: "How many men, in fact, who had ceased practicing, who had no longer come to our churches, have quickly invaded them from the first days of the alert. Openly or in secret, they have put their consciences in order; very many have received in their hearts the God of the strong." He exulted: "Faith was not dead at all, only numbed; a moment of surprise was sufficient to stimulate it and make it active."[22] After describing a full church near the opening battlefields of the Meuse, he states: "We complain, we clergy, of not having enough men in our churches, and then the war arrived with its threats, its dangers, with death which reaps our ranks without ceasing, reduced human respect and resuscitated the somnolent faith."[23] In fact, he predicted "the war will make France more pure; it will destroy all that divides it, to make it one in generosity, in heroism; it will make reign, after the brotherhood of arms, social brotherhood, *l'union sacrée.*"[24]

Most of the chaplains were happy to assign responsibilities to the soldier priests, nurses, and stretcher-bearers when they could. In fact, without their help, the chaplains could not have managed to reach as many of the wounded and dying as they did. Abbé Achille Liénart's journal provides an example of this division of work. He explained that when he arrived at his new post at Champigny near Reims as volunteer chaplain on Holy Thursday, April 1, 1915, his first care was to organize possible confessions and Easter communions. His military parish included a regiment, the 102nd Territorial, which was in reserve, and another, the 274th, which was in the trenches, and the cavalry of Courcy. He quickly found that there were two soldier priests in the unit in the trenches, including the Jesuit Pierre Durouchoux, and one in the reserve unit. These priests could help him to the extent that their superiors would allow. He said he was the most mobile, so he took care of the most isolated detachments and assigned the others to the soldier priests.[25]

Stretcher-bearers and nurses repeatedly expressed their desire for greater opportunities to serve the men as priests. Many voiced complaints in their memoirs and letters about the lack of opportunity. Teilhard de Chardin described the situation most graphically in a letter to his cousin from Rexpo-ede in the Nord on May 28, 1915. He stated that there is seldom an attack, but when there is, "work piles up and has to be done in a hurry, and necessarily. I fear, in a very mechanical way—the occasions when one has to bring in the badly wounded are comparatively rare, and I missed many." He felt helpless in dealing with colonial (Moroccan) troops, he explained, because of the difference in language and mentalities. He lamented: "In the end, accordingly, it has only been with occasional individuals, officers particularly, that I have been able to act as a priest; it is true that a single minute of such occasions, when you feel as needed and, through his help, as strong as our Lord, makes you forget the long periods of inactivity and justifies weeks of waiting and of life apparently turned to no account."[26]

By Christmas 1915, he was encouraged again. He wrote from Agincourt, on December 24:

> First of all, let me tell you that we too are going to have our Christmas celebrations. At the spontaneous request of the officers and men, I shall be saying midnight mass in the village church very beautifully decorated by the daughter and son from the chateau, with whose help,

too, I have been able to teach the men some carols;—apple tarts, cleverly baked by two of my *poilus* are waiting in the room next door to appear at *réveillon*. ... What more do we need to forget for a few moments the war and the trenches we'd be floundering in at the moment but for the sudden change that sent us off to the rural depths of the Pas de Calais. As I see it, this Christmas that is not without some religious feeling, is an opportunity to be eagerly grasped of appearing openly as a priest before the new draft in the regiment, the officers particularly, with most of whom (the new ones, I mean) I haven't yet made the full contact that will no doubt be found this evening at the C.O.'s table. Pray that I may acquire and exercise a sanctifying influence on these men, more than one of whom I shall probably see die.[27]

Soon, he was complaining again about the difficulties of practicing his ministry. From Eisnes, on June 19, 1916, he wrote: "[W]hat has so far marked my time in the Verdun area (now nearly finished) has been a sort of moderate degree of danger without the consolation of apostolic work or the occasion to show any particular devotion to duty. Nothing to really arouse or spur on the will or make it vibrate in tones of unsuspected richness."[28]

Assigned as a nurse in Salonika from February 1916 to July 1917, thirty-eight-year-old Georges Sevin, son of a blacksmith from a small town near Orléans, had been mobilized in January 1915 from his parish in a small village in northwest France near Pithiviers. He wrote to his mother that he was upset because there seemed to be discrimination against Catholics. The times allotted for mass, he complained, were inconvenient, especially for receiving communion. He was assigned general chores by the major, who scolded him for the fault of being too occupied with religion.[29]

Albert Bessières, a thirty-seven-year-old Jesuit stretcher-bearer who had been exiled with other Jesuits in Belgium since September 1901, was mobilized from his position as professor at a novitiate in Saint-Heeren-Elderen, near Tongres. He complained in December 1914 that he was assigned to construct huts and dig ditches along with seven other priests who were hospital attendants. Doctors and dentists were assigned to duties suitable to their skills, while priests were not, he said. He had had high hopes to serve the troops' needs as a priest and complained that the War Ministry was doing nothing for the spiritual well-being by assigning priests in this fashion. He wrote: "What have we done for the advancement, for the support of spiritual powers on which rests the moral dynamism of the nation? What have we done so that all the priests of France, representatives of these powers, may provide, both in the interior and at the front, all the services that the nation has the right to expect from them right now? Should our allies and even our enemies be able to give us some opportune lessons in this as in other matters?" He felt that priests in the war were following their own "way of the Cross."[30]

Priests who were fortunate enough to be assigned the role that is most common for a priest in war, that of chaplain, naturally had their apostolic mission in the forefront of their minds. Their estimates of their impact on the troops varied with both their personalities and their assignments. Their work prospered under those military superiors who were indulgent, but not under others. In every case, however, their ability to meet the religious needs of the soldiers suffered mightily because of the demands of the war itself and the conditions of the battlefield.

Echoing the sentiments of Abbé Castelin's letter to *La Croix*, the Franciscan monk Édouard de Massat, who had worked against many obstacles to obtain his appointment as chaplain, was enthusiastic about the religious revival he witnessed at the front. He wrote to his sister in November 1914:

> Oh! The war, death, which every day takes several of us, is a missionary whose voice is more eloquent than our own. There is no lack of matter for serious reflection for me and for them [the soldiers], the most beautiful and best of books; it is often shown in eyes full of tears and broken hearts. I believe truly, in seeing the renewal of Christian life in our soldiers, that France will come out of this struggle of giants, not only with increased territory, but with a new soul.[31]

From a bourgeois family in the Department of Loir et Cher in central France, grandson of a senator from the Sarthe, Louis Lenoir had been exiled from France with the other Jesuit seminarians to complete his years of theology at the Jesuit seminary in Hastings, England. When war was declared, he was a professor in a Jesuit school in Belgium. He had been assigned to the auxiliary service, so he did not have to return to Paris as soon as he did. In his eagerness to volunteer to be a chaplain, he caught one of the last trains out of Belgium in the face of the invading Germans, and had to go part of the way on foot. He arrived at his family home in Versailles and, despite the advice of his rector, began immediately to look for a position as chaplain. There were many others in competition but after a number of failed attempts with the Health Service, he received an assignment as an official chaplain in the first colonial corps upon application to General Colonna de Gioveltina, its superior commander. He was warned that this post was extraordinarily dangerous because these troops would be sacrificed first. Nonetheless, he eagerly embraced the assignment and left on August 11, 1914, for the east where the colonial corps was united with the Fourth Army in Lorraine.[32]

One of the most legendary chaplains, Lenoir came to be emblematic of the dedication and fearlessness of military chaplains in bringing religious succor to the troops. He is memorialized in the Army Museum in Les Invalides. His clerical garb and portable altar are ensconced there amongst other items documenting the war.

After the first Battle of the Marne, he wrote to his parents that he was the happiest and the most fulfilled he had ever been:

> [T]he days and nights are filled by a nearly uninterrupted apostolic work and a thousand times more consoling than I had hoped. Grace works marvels in our poor soldiers; I have already given several thousand individual absolutions, without counting the general absolutions. Since August 22nd, there have hardly been ten men who have refused absolution. They are returning to God with feelings of faith and contrition that they seem never to have abandoned. If these consolations did not include so many sorrows, separations, ruins, atrocities of all sorts, I would now be living in the happiest period of my life. Alas! It is also the most anguished, the most odious. I always see bodies in pieces in the fields, clusters of human remains, villages in flames, where, under the uninterrupted noise of the cannon, we search for the wounded. But I always also hear their calls for a priest, I always feel on my cheek their last tearful kisses, where their whole soul passes; for I am for them all their absent loved ones: father, mother, wife, fiancée; they tell me everything, as if they are talking to their loved ones whom I personify in spite of myself, with what feelings![33]

Capt. Frédéric de Bélinay, a Jesuit who had been mobilized as a lieutenant, provided a description of his amazement at Lenoir's success. He had arrived three weeks before Easter one Sunday in 1915, to say mass in the Church of Courtémont in the area of Champagne-Ardenne and the district of Saint Menehould. It was full of colonials and they were receiving communion. He was surprised to see this and when he asked another priest about it, he was told that it was the work of Père Lenoir. Belinay wrote: "This poor Jesuit had developed an influence over the colonials that had to be seen to be believed. . . . These souls, uncouth and sometimes depraved, often ignorant of any basic knowledge of religion, open to his influence by the charity of a saint, give themselves over to this belated grace, with the eagerness of neophytes marked for death. These men do not climb out of the trenches anymore to leave for an assault without having received communion."[34]

Bélinay provided a physical description of Lenoir, his attraction for the soldiers, and his remarkable ability to make every person feel very special. He said Lenoir was rather small and looked about nineteen years old: "Behind his spectacles, his brown eyes glowed with kindness, interest, and devotion. His face was mobile, expressive, and always smiling. He had this power of kindliness, which was one of the strengths of Saint Francis Xavier. Fatigue, *cafard* [this expression was used to describe profound battle fatigue and depression experienced by all the soldiers], exasperation vanished when he turned toward you the enchantment of his abundant charity."[35]

Thirty-four-year-old Abbé Marcelin Lissorgues, of the diocese of St. Flour, left as a volunteer chaplain of the 165th Division in 1916 when that unit was created. His journal covers twenty-three months at the front and four after the armistice, during which time he served with three different infantry regiments on battlefields in the region of the Aisne, Verdun, and the Oise. He had been a priest since 1903 and was the director of *La Croix de Cantal*, one of the regional newspapers of *La Croix*. Some of his journal was published during the war in that newspaper. In fact, the main purpose of his journal seemed to be to inform those on the home front of the conditions under which the soldiers served. Jean Norton Cru described his journal as one that indicated a good understanding of the life of the men and explained it better than others.[36]

His apostolic interests are clear, however, when he rejoices to see men crowding the churches. In an entry for February 25, 1916, he wrote: "Nothing is more deeply moving, nothing stimulates the most profound reflections as much as the gruff voices of the men, expressing to God their hopes, their anxiety, their resolute bravery. I have seen, in the interior, too many Churches where men leave to the women the care of praying to God, to not be pleased here at these virile assemblies, where no woman appears, and where there are not only men assembled, but heroes."[37]

Abbé Liénart, serving as an unofficial volunteer chaplain in the opening days of the war, recounted his responsibilities during a period of inactivity following a forced retreat from the Germans in Belgium, from September 15 to November 21, 1914. He wrote: "I was at the same time the chaplain of the camp and the curé of the village. Each day there was a benediction of the Holy Sacrament with a sermon which drew both civilians and military men, and I was the happy witness of a real religious renewal among very many souls."[38]

The Parisian pastor Abbé Pierre Lelièvre, serving as volunteer chaplain in the regiments of the 19th Infantry Division, described being overwhelmed with the religious response of the soldiers during the Artois offensive. He wrote:

> In all my life as a priest, I cannot find a single day which resembled even a little those days of the 6, 7, and 8 of May, 1915. I visit nearly every regiment and nearly all of the men come to the chaplain, either in a corner of a trench, or in the first shell hole that is available. . . . They all come; peasants, nobles, industrialists, professional noncommissioned officers, fathers of families, and as they humble themselves before God admitting their faults, so mild in my opinion, and pardoned in advance, because of the offering they are making, all, all tell me: "Yes, yes chaplain, it is with all my heart, with all my heart." Some of them add: "It is hard all the same, because of my wife and children." Then, as I weep with them and as I lean my head on their shoulders, they repeat, "But it is with my whole heart, chaplain, with my whole heart." Then they leave . . . I did not see them again.

He added: "Truly I hate war, no one can hate it more, I believe. Nonetheless, I have blessed it sometimes, during these three days when I have seen it raise humble souls even to the heights of Christ on the Cross."[39]

As the war inexorably continued, the priests expressed fewer romantic notions that their presence on the battlefield would lead to the permanent reconversion of France. As they dealt with more situations, they seemed to look at their opportunities with a greater realism. They often fluctuated between enthusiasm and discouragement, depending on the situations they faced. Nonetheless, they persisted in their efforts to find opportunities to provide priestly succor to their comrades and to convert them, despite feeling the same kinds of battle weariness as their fellows.

Seminarian Jean Nourisson's hopes began to be mingled with serious doubts that the religious revival would continue after the war. In a letter dated April 23, 1915, just after he left for the front, he engaged in a long discussion of whether or not there is a true religious revival. He was surprised to see that many colleagues quoted in the *Faisceau* (letters from Sulpicians published and distributed to colleagues at the front and at home) enthusiastically believed in it. He elaborated in his next letter, dated April 29, that he feared when the men no longer faced death, most of them would revert to being "slaves of wine and of the flesh."[40]

Later he again tried to find evidence for hope. In his letter of June 25, 1915, he wrote that he did not think the war would continue another winter, but he feared for the future. Then he stated: "If there would be a real return to God, the war would finish quickly, and that would be the Golden Age. But will it happen? Here we have the regiments of the IX Corps. They have an entirely remarkable Jesuit chaplain, whose work has evidently been profound. He has a beautiful effect on these young people. In the evenings, the Church is full and they sing with a conviction that I have never seen elsewhere. Every morning, there are many soldiers at mass and very many receive daily communion. If this were true everywhere!"[41]

Teilhard de Chardin's letter of May 28, 1915, to his cousin Marguerite, reflects a sense of realistic accommodation and continued determination:

I am greatly struck by this double fact: the very small number of souls in whom the need for religion has awoken, and the extraordinary vulgarity that goes with this atrophy. The Christian souls in my circle are very few in number, but it is as clear as daylight that they are, with rare exceptions, the only ones that are "fulfilled," the only ones that are truly human. And so the apparent failure of religion is in reality a triumphant vindication of the need of it and its effectiveness. May I confess, just to your ears, that at times I feel terribly tired of the selfish, bourgeois (to put it no worse) surroundings I am imprisoned in? At such moments I long to dismiss all this world to its bottles or its bunk and build myself an ivory tower. But, from the Christian angle, that would be shameful. Did our Lord do anything but step down and teach us? I must remain on good terms with the "common herd" and keep contact with it. Pray that God may help me to do so.[42]

Periodically Teilhard de Chardin seemed overcome with surprised indignation and discouragement at the complete lack of religious influence, which he described among the population. He wrote from Bagneux, Marne, on January 25, 1917, when he had reached the end of a long march and the front was still far in the distance. They did not know what the future would hold—neither the poilus nor the higher ups. He wrote:

> During our last days on the road, through a very bad country from the religious point of view, I had the opportunity, in talking with the people and parish priests, to gain a certain amount of human experience. You can't imagine the revolting states of selfishness, ill nature, meanness, and human pettiness to which these peasants are reduced, deprived of religion and educated on the state's republican principles! It's an unanswerable condemnation of "laïque" [secular] morality even from the natural and positivist point of view. I've never yet come into contact, so palpably, with the real decomposition of humanity that comes from the disappearance of religious feeling.[43]

Although sergeant-nurse Abbé Bourceret wrote of conversions and expressions of piety, he also was periodically discouraged. By March 1915 he complained that the prodigious conversions of the first days of the war had disappeared.[44] In July 1915 he disagreed with the curé he served under in Paris, who believed that the religious revival would last. He wrote that men became accustomed to death when surrounded by it. He asked: "Do you think, your reverence, that they have worked for so many long years . . . to destroy religious sentiment in several generations that one war would be enough to bring it back to life? That would be too beautiful and too easy."[45]

Even Abbé Lenoir, whose successes with missionary activities were legendary, had times of serious discouragement. Between June and September 24, 1915, the troops he worked with were at rest. He wrote: "The nonchalance of these men is unbelievable and saddens me. If you knew what anxiety overwhelms me and what *cafard* as well sometimes! . . . The ignorance or indifference of the masses, hostility of some. . . . And death is very near!"[46]

He was hoping, he wrote to his friend, that the special ceremonies planned for the feast of the Assumption of the Blessed Virgin Mary on August 15 would "shake off this lethargy." Instead the central celebrations planned could not take place because they were ordered to occupy a sector very disadvantageous for apostolic work. They would be in a forest of oaks, separated from the Germans by a swamp, but spread out considerably. It was impossible for the men to come to him for communion. He planned at first to multiply the number of masses and the leaders of the battalions supported him. But this was not to be. He wrote despairingly to his friend of his profound sense of inadequacy. He lamented:

> Why this curse of the Good Lord on our August 15th celebrations? Why were hundreds of souls who may in several days appear before Him not able to come? The Assumption must have prepared them for it; no feast will replace it from here on. And then?—I ask myself what has been the obstacle to the necessary graces; and I have a great, great fear that it is me. If you knew, dear good friend, how inferior I am to the task. In this very special *milieu* anyone would have done ten times more than I have done. Now more than ever I feel powerless, incapable, I do not know what to do or say; both vis-à-vis Our Lord and vis-à-vis the soldiers, I am paralyzed—and I know that a terrible accounting will be asked of me, that I will not be able to give. Pray very much, very much for me, excellent friend—not because of me, I am not worth it, but for my poor *Marsouins* [colonials], whose souls I am not saving.[47]

His biographer, Guitton, asserted that his discouragement did not last long. It was mitigated by the devotion of some other soldiers, new converts and others to whom he was able to bring communion.[48]

In that same year, twenty-four-year-old chaplain Abbé André de La Barre de Carroy supported Lenoir's complaint, claiming that during a rest period in a large village, "there is no one left but a dubious population of profiteers and exploiters of the weakness of solders." The soldiers had full purses and plenty of temptations, and frequented the cabaret more than the church. When La Barre would run into them on the street, he would ask what had become of them, trying to be tactful. Once they were back in the battlefield near the enemy, he observed, "the ceremonies remained beautiful and numerous, the apostolate fruitful."[49]

La Barre, son of Comte de La Barre, a cavalry officer, had been discharged for reasons of health before the war, but did not want to stay behind when other priests were going to war. He was accepted as a volunteer chaplain and was sent first to Châlons-sur-Marne with eleven other priests engaged as he was. He received his assignment at Bar-le-Duc to the 4th Corps, Quartier Général, at Romagnes-sous-Montfaucon. By 1915 he was serving with the 102d Infantry Regiment and was killed shortly thereafter. A witness described him as going by reading his breviary on his way to visit the trenches and being hit by a shell at Jouchery (Marne) on July 26, 1915.[50]

In his war journal, Abbé Jean Lagardère explained that even during the opening days of the war the men lost their interest in religion when they left the front lines. He wrote: "Religious in the trenches, but at twenty kilometers from the line of fire the men amuse themselves and only practice religion, at least most of them, according to their upbringing: 'One cannot change hearts very easily.'" He pessimistically asserted: "The depths of latent paganism are always ready to be revived by the push of irreligion descended from the popular sectors, where it stirs up envy and hatred."[51]

Lagardère fluctuated between this skepticism and encouragement, influenced by daily experiences and conditions throughout the war. He rejoiced during the Battle of the Marne in the spring of 1915: "Souls fall like ripe fruit."[52] And again on All Saints Day, November 1, 1915, when he declared he was able to exercise a "noble and fruitful ministry." He recounted that he spoke in the open air with an eloquence that made his audience weep. He had heard the confessions of numerous soldiers. He described the men as weeping after confession and absolution and asking him to accompany them to the trenches. He wrote: "It is here and not in the hospitals that we belong: it is near the living, under machine-gun fire, that our example would be comforting and transforming."[53]

After he had returned from the front because he was wounded, volunteer chaplain Abbé Lelièvre wrote an entry in his journal on July 22, 1917, that expressed a more cynical attitude toward the ultimate impact of the war on religious practice. He wrote that there were revelations to a peasant woman that were received by the archbishop of Paris and the president of the republic stating that France could be saved only if the image of the Sacred Heart was put on the flag of France.[54] He commented rather sarcastically, if realistically: "Well, if that was true, if the Sacred Heart placed this impossible condition on his intervention in favor of our cause, I would be even more pessimistic and I would conclude that France is lost. For official France has hope only in force and no ideal but interest in pleasure."[55]

Other priests, however, like Abbé Achille Liénart, later bishop of Lille, never seem to have experienced disillusionment. He never complained of a lack of religious devotion among the troops for whom he served as volunteer chaplain. He very assiduously performed his duties throughout the entire war and seemed always to have a balanced, realistic approach. His journal entry for November 1914 was very similar to his journal entry for Easter 1917. In the first, he stated that he provided services for the civilians and military and was the happy witness of a religious renewal in many souls.[56] And still at Easter 1917 he speaks of a good number of confessions and communions.[57]

Priests and seminarians, whether they served in combat or noncombat positions, as infantry, stretcher-bearers or chaplains, all hoped and planned to evangelize their fellow soldiers. Before the war, many had come to realize how much the Church had neglected the new industrial classes and had failed to develop new ways of outreach. Although some of them, particularly the youngest, entered the barracks with some trepidation, they seemed acutely aware of the opportunity to meet men who had little previous acquaintance with religion. For some of them, this possibility was their justification for being in the war at all. It assuaged the guilt they could not help but feel for the moral jeopardy in which it placed them.

Because there were so few chaplains, each of these priests was needed and found at least some opportunities to serve their fellow soldiers in a religious capacity. Their tales of ministry during impromptu situations fill their memoirs, and were often quoted in the Catholic press. Their descriptions of their unusual opportunities in the chaos of war to evangelize men who were not the usual churchgoers in early twentieth-century France highlight a remarkable aspect of the war experience, unique to these men, and important to the history of church-state relations. They demonstrated ingenuity in the face of overwhelming obstacles stemming from the exigencies of the war, military regulations, or unsympathetic commanders. Although they were realistic enough to have doubts about the lasting effects of the war on religious observance, they never allowed discouragement to lessen their determination to be convincing ambassadors of the faith.

When he wrote a memoir based on his journal nearly forty years after the war, Léonce Raffin, stretcher-bearer and later chaplain, was able to conclude, in hindsight, that the law that drafted priests into the army had indeed provided an opportunity, unforeseen by the anticlericals who adopted it. It gave "a new field of action to priests, in the barracks first, then in the armies, these soldier priests were going to penetrate the most diverse milieu and make contact with an entire group of young people who had not previously known anything about them."[58]

In addition to providing this opportunity for them to have access to more French men than ever, the war provided the opening for them to prove that they were just as patriotic as every other Frenchman, "like the others," as Teilhard de Chardin would assert. After years of being pariahs or being exiled, this roused their hopes and dreams about once more being integrated into French society. Their doubts about going to war as clergy were mitigated by these aspirations, as well as by the approval of the Vatican and their bishops. Their experiences at the front surprised and changed them. This transformation is described in the following chapters.

CHAPTER FOUR

PRIESTS AS PATRIOTS AND WARRIORS

Although military service was imposed on the French clergy by the military laws of 1889 and 1905, their letters, journals, and biographies indicate they embraced the opportunity. Bishops and the Catholic press seized on examples of the clergy's courage and self-sacrifice at the front to prove the Church's loyalty to France in the face of continued anticlerical disparagement. The men themselves expressed a sense of duty and patriotism and a longing to participate with their fellows. Priests and bishops alike found it easy to justify the war in the face of German aggression. They believed the cause of France and its allies to be "right" and "just." This helped them to rationalize their participation in the war.

Many of the priests entered the barracks with trepidation and were surprised by their affinity for the discipline and order of military life. They enjoyed their newfound camaraderie with their fellow soldiers, whose bravery and courage they admired. They were even more astonished with their reactions to battle and their embrace of violence. Even chaplains occasionally were caught up in the spirit of battle, and in a number of incidents actually led the troops when their commanders were killed in the midst of battle. Chaplains fused religious and patriotic sentiments with apparent ease, finding ways to make patriotism a Catholic value. Their help was much appreciated and rewarded by commanders.

There was no sign of pacifism among these priests; nevertheless, they did not deny the horrors of war or refrain from criticizing military strategies that led to slaughter. Some articulated their continuous moral struggle between the values of their priesthood and the duties of a soldier. Nonetheless they found comfort and sought to comfort others with the religious ideal of self-sacrifice, modeled by Jesus Christ.

Their battlefield experiences would bring combatants and noncombatants alike a profound realization of their own humanity in the face of the violence of war. It engendered in them a strong sense of brotherhood and identification with their fellow soldiers and their country. Their dilemmas and accommodations seem strange to the twenty-first-century reader, accustomed to consider the role of priest as one of peacemaker, not warrior. They provide us with another profound example of the impact of war on the human psyche.[1]

Despite the conflict with moral and canonical law posed by the role of priests in the military, both the hierarchy and the Catholic press touted the heroism of the *curé sac au dos* (priest with a pack on his back). From the very beginning of the war, both diocesan and national Catholic newspapers published letters recounting the exploits of priests at the front. They used statistics both to prove Catholic patriotism and to combat various rumors spread to impugn the hierarchy and the clergy: that the Church hierarchy had wanted the war and had even given money to the Kaiser; that clergy were *embusqués* (shirkers), while fathers of families were dying at the front.

A number of books, published in the middle of the war, portrayed the priests' death on the battlefield as glorious sacrifice for God and country. They may have been propaganda, but they did provide verifiable stories of the priests on the battlefield. Two examples of such writing were: René Gaëll's *Les soutanes sous la mitraille, scènes de la guerre*, published in Paris in 1915, and *Impressions de guerre de prêtres soldats*, edited and published in Paris in 1916 by the Jesuit editor of *Études*, Léonce de Grandmaison.

Mgr. Hector-Raphael Quilliet of Limoges provides an extreme example of the lengths to which the bishops went to defend their priests and themselves from accusations impugning their patriotism. After enduring the publication of several articles calling into question both his own patriotism and that of the priests of his diocese, in December 1915 Mgr. Quilliet wrote a response to the offending local newspaper, *Le Populaire du Centre*. These articles had accused the priests of shirking the battlefront, calling them embusqués. They claimed that priests refused to become volunteer chaplains, when Quilliet had put out a call for them, because they would not be paid. If actually mobilized, priests received assignments in hospitals away from the front lines or in bureaucratic jobs with the High Command. Quilliet refuted these charges in a fifteen-page letter and demanded that it be published. The editor refused to publish it in its entirety and Quilliet sued before the correctional tribunal of Limoges and won a judgment against the newspaper.

Quilliet quoted the newspaper as stating that priests were not numerous at the front. The bishop mocked the editors for earlier demanding that the front be laicized, but now, that priests be sent into the trenches in the name of equality. He asserted that his clergy had experienced many casualties between September 1914 and October 1915: four killed, four disappeared in combat, one taken prisoner, and several wounded. They had received eleven citations and two had received the Cross of the Legion of Honor.[2]

The priests, for their part, were motivated, like many other Frenchmen of the period, with a sense of duty and patriotism. Although the call to war was inconvenient for the stretcher-bearer Teilhard de Chardin, he wanted to be "like the others." He interrupted his studies at the Sorbonne to join two of his brothers at the front. Two more brothers were in training, and the youngest but one of his six brothers had just been killed. He wrote that he believed the war was "a baptism into reality" for soldier-priests, "a great human experience, a chance to act as a person in relation with men whose life he was sharing."[3]

Youngsters like the eighteen-year-old seminarian Marcel Baillat were very convinced of their duty to come to the aid of their country. He wrote to an unnamed confidant at the beginning of the war: "I believe that it is my duty and I will do it. I want to be a priest and if I do not die very soon, nothing, you understand, absolutely nothing will stop me; but my country has need of me and I will go, it is my duty right now."[4]

Even noncombatants expressed a great deal of patriotic fervor. The forty-four-year-old Abbé Bourceret, although assigned as a nurse, was captivated by emotions of patriotism at the beginning of the war. While he was with troops preparing to move to the front, he watched the soldiers passing in review before the commandant and cried out: "Forward! After the Teuton! We have to conquer them. Henceforth only our victory will prevent them from doing harm. Forward!" He reflected that they were marching against "the horrible Boche who have so profoundly humiliated us in 1870, who have frequently provoked us since; against the German, prolific and invasive race, overproud and brutal, barbarous in spite of 'la Kultur' which it glorifies and which it would like to impose on the entire world."[5]

Patriotism overwhelmed Gabriel Chevoleau's complaints about the blasphemies and the daily noise to which he was subjected in the barracks. The twenty-eight-year-old seminarian from La Rochelle was patriotic from his origins in the Bocage of the Vendée, according to his biographer. He had not been in military service before the war, but responded with enthusiasm to the call of his country. When he was sent first to Flanders, later to Verdun, that patriotism resounded in his first letter to a friend: "Here I am a soldier of France, one of the units on which rests a little the salvation of the country. I feel proud to wear the uniform. I would profoundly prefer the other uniform; for I was born instead for peaceful conquests; but, since it is necessary . . ." And indeed he proved to be a brave soldier, dying in battle leading a squadron near Verdun in 1916.[6]

Priests from Alsace and Lorraine, ceded to Germany after the French defeat in 1870, were often highly motivated by patriotism. In his introduction to the memoir of officer Abbé Jean Julien Weber, Mgr. Joseph Doré, bishop of Strasbourg, explained that Weber, an Alsatian, was imbued with a strong sense of nationalism and raised on the patriotic hymns of Paul Déroulède.[7] Xavier Thérésette's biographer also believed that the seminarian's Alsatian mother had inspired him from a young age with an "ardent patriotism, which distinguished the faithful populations of the annexed provinces."[8]

Of course, it did not take a person's origins to dream of *revanche* (revenge) for the ignominious defeat of 1870 and the loss of the territories of Alsace and Lorraine. The young seminarian Bernard Lavergne wrote to his father from his barracks on July 28, 1914, that he believed, from the dispatches coming from Austria, that war would be declared. He said that he looked forward to *revanche* for the old wound to France. Proud to have a military career like his father, he asked: "Give your blessing to your youngest son who is nearly in arms." Then on July 30 he wrote: "We are waiting from one minute to the next for the publication of the order of mobilization. . . . We are working vigorously while waiting to activate the tremendous machine. It will be an instrument of Providence, of God's Justice and Goodness: certainly of his Goodness, but perhaps while breaking some windows. . . . May the good Angels of France watch over us."[9]

Jesuit seminarian René de la Perraudière wrote that he was thrilled when he learned on February 25, 1916 (by then he was a sergeant) that his regiment was being sent to participate in the defense of Verdun. He had written a few days earlier: "Oh! to be one of the French who will enter Metz! What can only be a hope now . . . but first and foremost: God's will be done! . . . faith! . . . That is the prayer of a simple Christian."[10]

Like many others in the Allied nations, the priests saw the war as justifiable in the face of an enemy who was defined as barbaric and pursuing world domination. They found proof in accounts of German atrocities: the invasion of Belgium and France without provocation, and the destruction of churches and libraries, even icons of civilization, like Reims Cathedral and the city and university libraries in Louvain, Belgium.

In a sermon in November 1914, Abbé Lenoir combined heartfelt patriotism with a critique of the past policies of the French government and a condemnation of German barbarism. He expressed the conviction that God would ultimately protect France, despite the fact that government policies had "systematically chased" Jesus Christ from the country. All the newly found devotion, the many confessions and communions at the time of All Saints Day (November 1), were signs that Christ had touched "our beloved *Patrie*." He continued: "And if our enemies have dared to aim their sacrilegious cannons at the cathedral of Reims, it is because there reside all the memories of the baptism of France, of the day when in beginning to be Christian it began to be grand. To destroy the baptistery of Clovis is symbolic for them; they hoped that the last sound of the bells of Reims, collapsing under the arches in flames, would announce to the world that France was dead." France had been asleep, he claimed, but now was the hour of reawakening: "By the grace of the all-powerful Christ, she [France] will end this war more alive than yesterday. What makes me certain is that I see Jesus Christ's work each day. Each day, touched, grateful, full of confidence, I see in your souls the resurrection of France."[11]

In the spring of 1915, the forty-four-year-old sergeant-nurse Abbé Bourceret expressed gratitude that he could be a part of the war, despite its horrors, because it was necessary to fight the barbaric German spirit, bent on world domination:

> If I did not go into the furnace of this war like the combatants, if I was not able to expose myself to the bullets and bayonets as they did,—my age did not permit it—at least I have been able to be near, to live this life even so, to partake of its dangers, to learn in this way, no matter how

imperfect, what war is able to be when science puts itself in the service of hate, when the barbarous Teuton assassinates for the pleasure of it, when he piles up ruins without rhyme or reason, when he destroys, under I know not what impulse, the most beautiful masterpieces of art, when he teaches us, better still by his literature, and despite its insolently written manifestos what his "Kultur" is worth. How right we were, oh how much, to fight with invincible tenacity against the Germanic spirit which would become "the rule of the world."[12]

By the time of his sermon on the first Sunday of Lent, March 12, 1916, as the troops were preparing to fight in the region of Verdun, Father Lenoir motivated the troops with a similar warning. He spoke on the Gospel of the temptations of Christ in the desert, comparing the plight of the troops with His:

Yes, you have suffered not for forty days, but for eighteen months, not only hunger, but cold, mud, ever-present death, in the desert of the heart, a very understandable weariness, especially among us Frenchmen, so brave, but so very tired! But duty calls, the situation imposed by the enemy. It is necessary to hold on no matter the cost. If the line yields, it is German domination, terrible! Or if because of weariness we accept peace before crushing the adversary, it will be necessary to begin again in ten years, you or your sons.[13]

Teilhard de Chardin, in a more philosophical statement, categorized the war as a "struggle between two moralities." In a letter dated January 16, 1917, he commented on the response the Allies had made to President Woodrow Wilson's request in December 1916 for both sides to declare their war aims as a first step to ending the slaughter. He wrote:

The Allies answer to Wilson . . . is surely excellent, for no cupidity shows through; but simply love of justice. . . . I see this document above all as a moral manifesto, something like civilized peoples' tables of traditional law. Germany must in the end declare her war aims too. And then she'll have to make her confession of practical faith in some sort of Nietzscheism, and so it will become abundantly clear that the present war is basically a struggle between two moralities. . . . It's Christian justice that we're fighting for.[14]

Although they went into the military out of duty and patriotism and a sense of opportunity for evangelizing their fellow soldiers, priests entered the barracks with some trepidation about remaining faithful to their vows and to their spiritual life. They were surprised, however, to find themselves very comfortable with military life and life on the battlefield. The war proved that clergy were especially suited to military duty by their clerical training and the virtues it cultivated. Despite the role ambiguity and the uncertainty of authority inherent in their situation in the war, they found the military regimentation to be quite like their previous life—instead of a bishop or a religious superior, there was a commanding officer; instead of the breviary, there was a regular military routine; instead of the camaraderie of the seminary, there was the bonding that came with life in the trenches.

Léonce Raffin, a stretcher-bearer and later volunteer chaplain, described the affinity between the required behavior of the soldier in war and the vow of obedience taken by members of religious orders: "For five years [of training] we have practiced this blind submission; and it is without doubt thanks to that that we have conquered. An order subject to dispute by those who would execute it is a compromised order; and a plan divulged too soon, a secret divulged, which risks reaching the vigilant ears of the enemy."[15]

Jesuit seminarian, corporal, then sergeant, René de la Perraudière wrote of the pleasure and comfort he took in army discipline, describing the feelings of patriotism and devotion it inspired in him: "I love it that we are made to polish up the regiment for two hours, to present arms, for two minutes to a brave soul who is decorated; and I also love a beautiful parade, in the open field, without spectators other than the General who inspects—because then one feels that one is working as a true soldier, purely for France . . . and for God, for in these cases, I try inwardly to march for Him."[16]

The military commanders demonstrated their recognition of this affinity in many ways. The most obvious is reflected in the swift promotion of the young men inducted under the auspices of the 1905 law, who were assigned combat positions. All ten of the combatant priests and seminarians under thirty whose memoirs or biographies I consulted were promoted to officer status in the opening months of the war. In his preface to René Gaëll's book, Gen. Victor Humbel applauded the bishops for allowing these promotions, stating: "Some bishops—these were, in my opinion, the most clear-sighted and the most prudent,—believed they should encourage their priests to obtain promotions to officer status. . . . Since they could not avoid military service why not profit from the superior instruction that they have received and the spirit of duty that animates them and which was strengthened in the seminary, to try to play a leadership rather than a subordinate role."[17]

The twenty-four-year-old Franciscan Xavier Thérésette's abilities were quickly realized by his superiors. Called up from the seminary in Belgium, he entered the barracks for two years of compulsory service in the "class" of 1911. He was a model of duty, quickly appreciated by his officers and promoted first to corporal, then to sergeant. When war broke out he was mobilized as a sergeant in the 164th Infantry Regiment, but promoted to second lieutenant in the 366th by November 3, 1914. His biographer claimed that he was a fervent patriot, who had a love for the military profession only surpassed by his vocation to the priesthood.[18] He was killed at the beginning of the offensive on Verdun, February 27, 1916, on hill 255, near Moulainville after nineteen months at the front. In his military citation of March 24, 1916, his superiors recounted that he was wounded leading a charge and kept fighting until he was wounded a second time. He refused help and told his troops to keep fighting and to not be taken prisoners.[19]

The forty-year-old Jesuit Pierre Durouchoux, scion of a Parisian military family, held the rank of sergeant in the territorial reserves at the beginning of the war. Called up in August 1914, he was sent home and started the procedure of applying to be a chaplain. But he was recalled by the end of September and made head of a section. In October 1915 he was promoted to lieutenant and then just a month and a half later, on December 1, 1915, he was promoted to the rank of captain. His numerous citations indicated that he was unfailingly brave but also a brilliant commander who provided "the most beautiful example of courage and duty." The citation of March 6, 1916, in particular, asserted that he was able to direct the men in difficult circumstances because of "the powerful moral influence that he always knew how to exercise on his troops."[20] After his death on the battlefield at Verdun on April 10, 1916, his men recounted that they loved and respected him for his calm and prudence. As befitting a priest, his concern for his soldiers' lives was remarkable for a World War I commander. His soldiers said he would study an order and determine how to succeed while sparing his troops as much as possible.[21]

Even the chaplains showed an affinity with military life. In the battlefield of Champagne on the third Sunday of September 1915, Lenoir urged his troops to obey their superiors without question. He said: "'To obey without seeking to understand.' Absurd pleasantry that should not be repeated! In certain cases when the motives of your superiors escape you, you are not able to understand the order, very well! But the order itself, its pronouncement, what the chief expects from you, you must always seek to understand it as well as you can, to assimilate it, to make it yours, in order to fulfill it with all your resources, to understand it with your intelligent initiative." Lenoir's biographer Georges Guitton commented that Lenoir certainly had not read Marshal Foch's *Principes de la guerre* but he echoed those principles in that sermon. Foch had said that it was better if the troops understood an order but to be disciplined is "to act on the orders that one receives, and to find their spirit and determine through reflection how they can be fulfilled." Lenoir, however, had found his inspiration in the writings of the founder of the Jesuits, Saint Ignatius.[22]

Beyond their comfort with military discipline, it is remarkable to find the combatant priests' enthusiastic reactions to battle. They themselves expressed astonishment. Capt. Frédéric de Bélinay explained the feeling to his fellow Jesuit, Teilhard de Chardin, in 1916 just after taking his final vows:

> Yes, I must confess that I'm almost frightened by the sense of fulfill-
> ment in every direction, provided by this profession (religious), by
> this intoxication of leading a company of picked troops under fire
> and taking a village. . . . All of my life I've had the painful feeling of
> being just a half-baked kid, and that the age of maximum vitality was
> going by without bringing me the manliness the lack of which is so
> noticeable, so undeniable, I mean so easy to put your finger on. And
> now the war brings me the lot. Whatever happens, I'll bless our Lord
> eternally for having let me see what I have seen, and for having given
> me this feeling of strength and confidence and the trust shown me by
> the men which is so moving.[23]

Bélinay was a descendant of a patriotic, noble family. Two of his brothers were in combat and his father, Maurice de Bonafos, Baron de Bélinay, left home in 1914 at the age of seventy-two to establish a hospital at Ussel with Red Cross volunteers. Bélinay himself had left Saumur as a lieutenant to join the Jesuits, but when war broke out, he returned to duty, accepting a commission as a cavalry lieutenant. He was promoted to captain in 1915.

Echoing Bélinay's feelings, the Jesuit Paul Dubrulle, a thirty-four-year-old second lieutenant, described the feeling of euphoria and camaraderie he felt leading his men in an assault during the Battle of the Somme: "At that moment I was bursting with admiration and enthusiasm. I felt that I was free and that I was a part of a superior being, immeasurably large, and a tiny atom lost in the ocean, I abandoned myself. Unconscious of myself, I was drawn as if by a magnet, into the fray, obsessed with the idea that the enemy was there and it was necessary to crush him."[24] He had served in the military prior to the war and left for Belgium to join the Jesuits. He too returned to take up his commission when the war began, serving in the battlefields in Champagne and Verdun. He was killed in a charge he led near Craonne on April 16, 1917.

Sergeant de la Perraudière wrote that he felt most alive on the battlefield. His letter of March 3, 1916, from the battlefields near Verdun, stated: "To tell you frankly about my morale, there are moments of fatigue when I see blackness. But three quarters and a half of the time, I am thrilled. Here, at least one lives, one feels oneself a combatant, a defender of the *Patrie*. And if that is very natural, I believe at least that it is not a bad feeling."[25] He too died on the battlefield March 8, 1916, at Verdun.

Teilhard de Chardin admitted to his cousin, Marguerite Teillard-Chambon, that after two and a half years at the front as a stretcher-bearer, he regretted choosing a noncombatant role. In a letter dated February 15, 1917, he wrote:

I assure you that I'd a thousand times rather be throwing grenades or handling a machine-gun than be supernumerary as I am now. What I'm going to say may not be very orthodox—and yet I believe there's a core of truth in it: I feel that doing so I would be more a priest. Isn't a priest a man who has to bear the burden of life in all its forms, and shows by his own life how human work and love of God can be combined? I'd be interested to know how many of us soldier-priests think the same. . . . I don't know whether I should react against this tendency. But I feel that I'm not being honest with myself unless I say what I think: if I said anything else, I'd be doing violence to my own self. Fundamentally, however, since we seem to be approaching the end of the war, it's really an academic question. But if I had to start again, I wouldn't take the line [choosing a noncombat position] I did in 1914.[26]

Perhaps even more surprising is that the chaplains too were often caught up in the fighting spirit. There are accounts of chaplains leading troops in assaults while on the front lines attending to the spiritual needs of the soldiers. On the Champagne front on September 25, 1915, Jesuit chaplain Lenoir began his usual visiting of all those who would go into battle first at 4 A.M. There was fog that morning and then a fine rain began, turning the mud viscous and heavy, making marching difficult. Lenoir followed the first wave to succor the wounded and the dying. The men had lost their commander during the assault and Lenoir found himself in the vicinity and "took command and lead the company to the assigned goal." He was wounded in the left thigh and refused the aide of the stretcher-bearers, saying that there were wounded who needed their attention more.[27]

Even Abbé Lelièvre, the Parisian priest, chaplain of the 10th Division, who called the war a "plague" in his memoir, led the troops to attack at Roclincourt during the offensive of Artois (May 9, 1915) when their officer threatened to shoot the troops for hesitating.[28] The Jesuit chaplain Paul Doncoeur also took command of several companies whose commanders were killed at Bouchavesnes on August 16, 1916. He had entered the Jesuit novitiate in 1898, and had studied theology in Jersey at the same time as Chardin. He was accepted as a volunteer chaplain at the beginning of the war and served throughout the war in a number of different units. According to his biographer, Doncoeur understood the companies were in great danger. If they did not advance they would soon be encircled and destroyed. Since he understood the plan of attack, he took measures into his own hands and, with him in the middle of "his soldiers," they seized the enemy trench, took more than one hundred prisoners, and neutralized the German positions. He was severely wounded himself, but urged the soldiers to keep on fighting, saying, "Hold on, no matter the cost."[29]

Doncoeur's reaction might be explained by his ancestry. He was the descendant of a Christian soldier, named "Doncoeur" by King Louis XI (St. Louis) himself during the Seventh Crusade. In her work on chaplains, Nadine Chaline explained that indeed, chaplains dealt with the issue of whether to draw a gun on the enemy according to their own character. She cited one example of a chaplain who claimed that he was overtaken by a kind of fever, a delirium, which made him determined to kill yet another "Boche" after he had killed the first.[30]

In his letter of June 10, 1917, from Paissy, stretcher-bearer Teilhard de Chardin did his best to explain what he regarded as the strange reaction he and his fellows had to the front lines. He wrote that currently his life was quiet and he had "a comfortable bunk in a wooded grove." He did not know if his regiment would be called to occupy a sector, but, he wrote: "If it is, I'll have no complaints: life in the saps and shell-holes has such a savour and tone that in the long run you find it difficult to do without it—although, at first, when you go back to it again, you count the days and hours till your relief."[31]

Not satisfied to be puzzled by his reaction, the philosopher in Teilhard de Chardin sought to explain it. On September 25, 1917, he wrote to his cousin from Muret-et-Croutes that he was proposing to the editor of *Études* that he would put his thoughts in writing in a work called "Nostalgia for the Front." He explained that he wanted to describe the feeling and provide some reasons for it. He wrote:

> The reasons, I believe, come down to this; the front cannot but attract us, because it is, in one way, the *extreme boundary* between what one is already aware of, and what is still in the process of formation. Not only does one see there things that you experience nowhere else, but one also sees emerge from within one an underlying stream of clarity, energy, and freedom that is to be found hardly anywhere else in ordinary life—and the new form that the soul then takes on is that of the individual living the quasi-collective life of all men, fulfilling a function far higher than that of the individual, and becoming fully conscious of this new state. It goes without saying that at the front you no longer look on things in the same way as you do in the rear: if you did, the sights you see and the life you lead would be more than you could bear. The exaltation is accompanied by a certain pain. Nevertheless it is indeed an exaltation. And that's why one likes the front in spite of everything and misses it.[32]

On October 4, he wrote that he had sent the article to the editor and had shown it to two friends, Beaugiard, in a colonial regiment, and a captain with whom he was friendly. Both men liked it. He continued, "By an odd coincidence, three or four days ago, two of my comrades (of very different moral calibre [sic]) invalided out because of wounds, confessed to me that the thought of the front made them feel homesick. This shows that the feeling of nostalgia that I've tried to analyze is very real and deep-seated."[33]

Even chaplains described these feelings of nostalgia when they were not at the front. During the course of leading the troops into battle on September 25, 1915, in the Champagne region, Lenoir was wounded in the thigh and sent to rest for at least three weeks. Although he remained active during his hospital stay, writing to many colleagues and soldiers, holding conferences among the hospitalized soldiers, he wrote of his boredom: "In the quiet, the nostalgia for the front roars." His anxiety to be back at the front increased each time mail arrived from his regiment, the 4th Colonial.[34]

On November 3, 1914, in the battlefields near Arras, the chaplain Lagardère decided to go at night to visit the trenches "to show the soldiers that the priest is with them everywhere, and to give them confidence, and also to tame the human body and to expiate sins of sensuality." He loved to do this and thought that to be an "apostle-soldier" was the best of all occupations in the world. Daily he participated in the peril of the trenches with the soldiers. He wrote: "Captain-chaplain savors these dangerous moments, and thanks God for permitting him to live through them escaping a fatal bullet."[35]

When his unit was sent to the Marne in January 1915, Lagardère passed a half day in the rear and returned to the front very quickly. He did not want to leave his post for an hour without necessity. He expressed his love for the front thus: "I am happy here: the friendship of the men, the rattling of arms, the noise of the cannon, the whistling of bullets, the view of the trenches, their infected mud delights me, thrills me, makes me quiver. I am only at home there, I only breathe there, I only do good there, I only feel myself a man there."[36]

There is little to no sign of pacifism in these memoirs, journals, autobiographies, and biographies of priests in the war. But there is no love of war for itself. Abbé Lelièvre comes the closest to pacifism in his statement in his journal in the Roclincourt area near Arras on March 15, 1916. He described a horrible attack resulting in many wounded and stated: "Ah! Horrible thing! And how I hate war. I hate it, to the point of surrendering forever every feeling of patriotism, if that could advance one hour the end of this abominable carnage."[37] Lenoir's biographer, Georges Guitton, stated that Lenoir had prayed that there would be no war: "Some days before the declaration of war, with the horizon already somber, he believed himself authorized to celebrate a votive mass for peace; and it is as a convinced pacifist that he praised the beauties of peace, with a kind of liturgical feast. . . . Like all Frenchmen in

1914 Father Lenoir . . . was very ready to avoid the plague that the Church in its litanies enumerates along with pestilence and famine, except at the price of honor."[38]

Although in other periods he wrote of his love of the front, the chaplain Lagardère expressed his horror at the effects of war during the battles he experienced in May 1917, in a "terrible sector" near Troyes. In a journal entry on May 9, he talked of burying twenty-one "of my children." One he described as being in sixty pieces found over two hundred meters of ground. "These are all Christ torn to pieces." On May 21, he described an attack in which there were so many wounded that they could not be transported: "I am going to the battlefield. Dead everywhere, a mountain destroyed, the image of the inferno, the wounded . . . buried by other bodies; I free one and then another. I return to the aide post and take up my work again: they identify the bodies, and when the last of the gravely wounded has disappeared, towards nine or ten o'clock, I return. . . . The war is a butchery."[39]

Nonetheless it was common for the priests to be appalled by pacifism, connecting it with socialism and lack of religious training. Abbé Bourceret commented on the fate of soldiers who were killed by their officers for refusing to fight. He wrote: "[I]t is unanimous to say that they were agents of disorder and that they have refused to go into battle." He then scolded the socialists: "Gentlemen leaders of antimilitarism, Gentlemen pontiffs of the *Internationale*, you have made a superb about-face, a skillful pirouette on the day of mobilization, but the seed you have criminally sowed among the people has borne its fruits. These condemned men, you condemn. You have been their evil genius. Whether you wish it or not, they are your victims. Their blood is on your head, historically and for eternity."[40]

Lenoir was dismayed by the idea that a soldier would wound himself to get sent back home. He recoiled when a doctor told him about such voluntary mutilations. On the Feast of Pentecost, 1915, he told the soldiers never to regard any wound as a "happy wound" if it took them away from the front. He said:

Reject still more, I beg you, as an expression of cowardice, these words which you often hear, 'the lucky wound.' Lucky, a wound that keeps you from defending your country for a long time? Lucky, a wound that deprives your regiment of a gun? Lucky, a wound that makes you useless to the sacred, pressing cause, which demands all our strength?

I do not want to hear these words among you; it is neither Christian, nor French. There is only one lucky wound, the one which allows you to remain at your post . . . ask the Holy Spirit for the strength to give . . . up to your last breath; and as long as you have blood in your veins, a little strength in your arms, make it bloom with the flowers of heroism and the fruits of victory for France.[41]

Nonetheless the priests were troubled repeatedly with something deeper and more personal, a confrontation with their own moral struggle, with their very human reactions to violence and war. Like Teilhard de Chardin, other priests and seminarians expressed ambivalent reactions to war and killing. They were shocked by their own response to killing and to being engaged in battle, and they openly admitted their feelings of ambiguity.

The youngest of them were very forthcoming about their moral struggles. In a letter dated August 31, 1915, written near the Artois front, the seminarian Cpl. Gabriel Chevoleau confessed that he suffered from feelings of despondency except when faced with danger. He illustrated with an example. He said that a young man from the Vendée on sentry duty called to him and told him to come and look. He could not see very well through the periscope, so he looked over the embankment and saw a German soldier digging a trench. The guard told him to get his gun, he did and aimed and the man fell. He described his feelings: "A kind of fierce joy, unknown and inexplicable, invaded my soul. It is frightening to see how much of Cain remains in each of us. Finally what do you think of that fact? Today my fatigue is dissipated."[42]

The Jesuit novice René de la Perraudière's biographer stated that he reflected on the position of a clergyman placed in the métier of a combatant. He says it was a problem, which posed itself "with sometimes frightening clarity." He confirmed: "He does not forget, he cannot forget that the Church wants its priests untouched by any spilt blood; he knows also that, if one can legitimately wish that the entire nation pay the cost of war, it is absurd to want all to pay in the same fashion. The priest and the future priest have a right to a special post, which without shielding them from the danger of shedding their own blood, does not submit them to the risk of shedding the blood of others."[43]

Although he would later embrace military life by agreeing to become an officer candidate in 1917, Jean Nourisson's troubled conscience is palpable in a letter to a friend at the end of October 1914: "These several days of physical rest with a little less boredom have raised my morale a little. This morning especially, I prayed more easily. In these times I voluntarily make the total sacrifice, but at other times I resign myself with difficulty to death under fire, especially to death with arms in my hand. I would go voluntarily under fire without arms, as a stretcher-bearer, and then fall! But this war is too horrifying and this bloody death is not that of a priest. It cannot be God's intention to allow priests and clerics to fight."[44]

Seminarian and corporal Marie-Bernard Lavergne expressed the same anxiety in his letter of January 20, 1915, to his sister Agnes from the barracks at Pelissier, before moving from his initial station at Rouen:

> The war we are going to make . . . if you knew the métier we have learned, whose tiniest details they have taught us! . . . This will be offensive war, incessant attack on entrenched positions; attack day and night and always with bayonets. What will be hard, finally, is to jump into one trench, then another to find men who will cry out perhaps on their knees: "Comrades! Comrades!" And then to have the instruction, the order, the duty to kill them all the same. . . . I do not fear death, but if it is necessary to get into a hand to hand fight, how will I close my eyes without seeing before me their mother, their wife, their children?

He asked her forgiveness for telling her these hard things, but trusted that she would still love him and understand. Then he said: "Pray for me. You see my whole soul in this letter, very calm to endure death, but anxious all the same with worry over causing death. Your prayer will be a balm for this wound, a ray of clear sunshine in this tempest." A letter on the following day to his brother André reflects similar sentiments. It seems, once he admitted his doubts to his sister, he could repeat them to his brother.[45]

Volunteer chaplain Abbé Marcelin Lissorgues's memoirs expressed horror at the violence of the war and scorn for those who had wanted war. Surrounded by the battlefields in the valley of the Aisne in April 1917, he reflected on the inherent contradiction between war and Jesus's greeting to his apostles after the Resurrection, "Peace be with you." He wrote: "To these men for whom war is a duty, how can I, oh my God, announce today the sweetness of your Gospel?" But then he found justification in the war for his troops, for himself, and for France: "The men do not make war for their pleasure. . . . The war is an evil worse than pestilence and famine. . . . Is not peace the principal aim of the war for the French? . . . The peace between peoples, the peace entwined with justice, we ask it of you, oh Sovereign Master of the Universe."[46]

Although not expressing the same level of internal conflict, other priests criticized strategy and even voiced questions over whether the sacrifice of so many lives was worth the small gains. Abbé Liénart described a series of fruitless attacks in a tight sector southwest of Reims between September 13 and 24, 1915, which resulted in a terrible bombardment of mines and shells, and many lives lost. He believed that these attacks had profoundly affected the morale of the men and asked: "What good is so much sacrifice for such a meager result?"[47]

Similarly he critiqued a mission they were required to fulfill on July 15, 1916, in the region of Verdun. His 28th Company received the order to attack an enemy post and to take prisoners so that the chiefs could identify the enemy divisions posted on the front and know exactly the importance of formations concentrated on Verdun. He recognized the mission had a real utility but said: "Our chiefs were mistaken in believing that these raids would fuel the offensive spirit among our soldiers. In reality these little operations cost us dearly and resulted in little gain, they depressed the soldiers' morale. Our raid of July 15 failed like the others, we had several wounded and we took no prisoners."[48]

In a chapter in his memoir entitled "La mort de la quatrième," the dedicated commander, Frédéric de Bélinay stated that he tried to tell his superiors that a planned attack was not a good idea. They were at the foot of hill 108 by the Aisne River. He wrote after an initial failed attack: "I wrote that the last failures had affected morale. The enemy, who just stopped the whole army corps dead, was not going to cede its trench to my company. We would take it without doubt, but in the counter attack, there was no section left in the whole brigade to support us. I only received a signed statement from the General of the division reiterating his order."

He continued: "These hours made me sad. For the first time in the war, I feared weakening. God being my only recourse, I wrote a card of consecration, which I have rediscovered, dated May 11, 17 hours, 25 minutes, 1917. At the moment of launching the attack I consecrated my exhausted and nervous company entirely to the Sacred Heart, asking Him, in memory of His agony, to give us the strength to do our duty, and to allow all our souls close to Him."

The attack succeeded, but he was wounded and only forty men remained. Nonetheless, he wrote: "But the present victory is formed by the integration of such sacrifices."[49]

Ultimately, priests found a way to integrate their religious values with those of the military. The thirty-four-year-old Jesuit chaplain Paul Doncoeur wrote that he was doing his best to help the regiment "regain its soul" while they were preparing for the battle for Reims and General Robert Nivelle's disastrous campaign at the Chemin des Dames in 1916. Perhaps his family heritage helped him to believe that encouraging the men as they prepared for battle was a religious occupation. He described praying for courage with soldiers who went into battle without enthusiasm.[50]

Abbé Liénart, too, said he helped men to face battle by religious means. He described in his journal the memory of an incident that took place in the area of Verdun that remained particularly dear to him. He served as chaplain to the 201st Infantry Regiment's first division, in the Plateau de Paissy sector between February 22, 1916, and July 23, 1916. He wrote that a Parisian of twenty, Henri Laplace, asked to prepare for first communion. He had been led by the example of his Catholic friends. Liénart prepared him and he received his communion.

Days later when Laplace was returning from Thiaumont, he met the chaplain and admitted that the violent bombardments were making him very afraid to complete the task of scouting out a position for his battalion. Liénart tried to calm him by explaining that he had just come from that way and had not been hurt. Then Liénart described that he realized reasoning was doing no good. He wrote:

> Happily, I was carrying the Blessed Sacrament with me. "Would you like to receive Communion?" I asked him. "So that you will be stronger." He agreed with pleasure. Then both of us kneeling, close together, beneath the shelling that was coming from all directions, I gave him Holy Communion. The change was immediate. He got back on his feet, confident and resolute, shook my hand and said to me: "Chaplain, I have no more fear, I am no longer alone since Jesus is with me, I will go on and if something happens to me, I am sure of going to heaven." Never have I better understood as I did in this instant the succor that Communion could give us no matter what duty we have to fulfill.

Afterward, Laplace did successfully accomplish his mission but a few days later, he was mortally wounded. Liénart saw him at the aide post of Bras and prepared him for death. He asked the priest to embrace him. Liénart reflected: "Jesus prepared him better than I did. Henri Laplace was not afraid of dying. He felt secure with Jesus."[51]

The priests often fused religious and patriotic sentiments with an admiration of battlefield spirit. The Jesuit chaplain Louis Lenoir wrote a letter to members of a society dedicated to Saint Francis de Sales describing an attack on April 13, 1915, when his troops were serving in the area of Le Fortin de Beauséjour: "This attack ... was splendid. From the start of the campaign, I had never seen anything so beautiful, so well led, so calmly heroic on everyone's part. The majority of the men who took part in the assault had first received Holy Communion, and very many had told me since: 'Never have I marched with so much courage, because I received the Good Lord and with Him, I felt stronger than everyone.' An officer who led the men and who died in the battle had cried out while going forward: 'Chaplain, we are having a great time!'"[52]

Officers appreciated that the priests were helping them inspire the troops. Lenoir was in the camps surrounding Sainte-Marie-au-Temple, between Amiens and Arras, in June 1915. The colonial corps was sent as reserve to the armies of the Nord. They were moved around quite a bit but then they were to be involved in the Champagne offensive under the direction of General Noël Édouard de Castelnau. The 4th Colonial was attached to the Second Army. In preparing for the offensive, they recommended that all the regiments multiply the reviews to exalt enthusiasm. Everyone from captains to generals wanted Father Lenoir for the task. Colonel Pruneau said, "I assure you that never can the head of a corps find an auxiliary as precious for the morale side of military education in time of war." In a letter of October 6, 1915, a nurse corroborated his words: "I ask God every day to preserve for the 4th at least its chaplain and its colonel; what would we do without these great leaders?"[53]

Almost all the priests found a moral justification for the war, a way to explain it to themselves and others that was based on their faith. Some of them found that the religious values of sacrifice helped them to rationalize the suffering at the front. They found it comparable to the sufferings of Jesus's crucifixion and death for mankind. To many of the priests it seemed that the soldiers and the priests were giving their life for both France and God. Combining patriotism and the Catholic faith seemed easy for most of them.

The 1915 Easter sermon of Abbé Louis Lenoir is one of the most precise explanations of the connection between religious faith, indeed the Catholic faith, and patriotism. His biographer, also a war chaplain, the Jesuit Georges Guitton, claimed the sermon provided "the central idea" of Lenoir's life and "the point of intersection between his religious and military apostolate." Lenoir told the gathered troops:

> The Catholic faith, in fact, tells a soldier what his duties are—duties of obedience to his chiefs, bravery in combat, endurance, total sacrifice of self for one's country—these are the sacred duties, from which he cannot escape without disobeying God Himself. . . . What's more, the Catholic faith—the *true* faith, that surpasses *actions*—gives a soldier the necessary comfort in the hours when his patriotism weakens. By prayer and confidence in God, by Holy [C]ommunion . . . it multiplies a hundredfold the courage of a man, and often makes a faltering man a hero. . . . Finally, the Catholic faith exalts patriotism, because beyond the supreme sacrifice it promises us a better life, infinitely happier than any here below, where with no separations, war, or tears, we will find again those we love whom death has temporarily separated us from.[54]

In July that same year, 1915, a few days after the Feast of the Most Precious Blood (July 1), Lenoir took the opportunity to explain the doctrine of "expiation." He discussed the contradiction between the fact that God had formally forbidden human blood sacrifice, yet allowed his only Son to be sacrificed to expiate the sins of humanity. And every day on altars all over the world, he told them, this sacrifice occurs again, covering the world with a "veritable flood where all the repentant are purified, where all heroism finds its strength, where every soul who wants to live can immerse itself and be reborn to the divine, immortal life." He then compared the French sacrifices with Christ's:

> Like that of Christ, this "beautiful blood of France" was today, as it has always been in history, "liberating blood" . . . spread across Europe and to the extremities of the earth to defend nations against injustice and support religious and social freedom. Plow the fields where the barbarian invasion was stopped, clear the ruins of Palestine or of Syria, search the plains of Poland, the beaches of Mexico and the United States, the mountains of Armenia, the perimeter of the Vatican, search all the

corners of the world where violated liberty has called for help, everywhere you will find traces of French blood. And now again, the river follows its normal course; if it has flowed to Jaulnay, to Massiges, to Beauséjour, it is both to save our country and the entire world from barbarism, it is to defend the law of God and the rights of people—that is our glory.... Also, my dear friends, at this hour when France asks for your blood, to continue its work, I beseech you to make it more pure, more rich, more generous, in mixing it once more with the blood of Christ.[55]

Ideas of warriors' sacrifice and expiation harken back to the period of the Crusades, according to Jonathan Riley-Smith. Preachers and popes regarded the sufferings of soldiers at war as holy; linked with Christ's sufferings on the Cross, they would have penitential merit.[56] And indeed some of the French priests preached that the sufferings on the battlefield would exonerate France's guilt for turning away from God. Priests saw in the wounded and dying soldiers the image of Christ crucified. Although this reasoning harkens back to the Crusades, only one of the priests I studied actually took inspiration from that period. From his youth, Édouard de Massat was captivated with Crusade imagery. His biographer claims that he chose to become a Capuchin because of that order's historical links with the Crusades, and with monastic orders such as the Knights Templar. He was thrilled by the idea of carrying the sword and taking holy orders as a standard bearer for Christ. At forty-four he had the opportunity to go into battle as a chaplain and enthusiastically followed the troops in their opening assaults, finally dying as he wished for God and France.[57]

The thirty-nine-year-old chaplain Abbé Charles Thellier de Poncheville, descendant of a noble family from the Nord, described his purpose in the battlefields of the Verdun area: "My task is to invigorate consciences weary with effort, perhaps troubled by the appalling killings. They will open themselves easily to thoughts, which justify the harsh conditions imposed by the defense of the country and of the program of humanity of which we are the guardians. In the radiance of the faith, the apparent grossness of our daily tasks is ennobled still more. Who can remain insensible in this place, at this hour, to the divine beauty of our doctrines of duty and sacrifice?"[58]

Léonce Raffin, who by 1916 was combining his duties as stretcher-bearer with those of an unofficial (bénévole) chaplain for an artillery unit in the 70th

Division, also compared the sacrifice of life on the battlefield to Christ's on the cross. In a sermon he gave at a mass requested for the anniversary of the death of an officer, just before his unit was leaving for Verdun in March 1916, he told the troops: "Maintain, gentlemen, the cult of our heroes! Imitating them will lead us to a double victory, that of France, which we want delivered from the Germans, and more prosperous than it has ever been, and also that of our souls, who, by the path of very often sad and bloody duty, prepare an eternal recompense before God."[59]

Teilhard de Chardin and De la Perraudière both commented on the problem for soldiers who lack faith to find meaning in the midst of horrible suffering and death. From Nieuport-Ville (Belgium) on February 2, 1916, Teilhard de Chardin wrote: "The men are suffering more than ever and accumulating the substance of inexpressible sacrifice. Why must it be that their agony should lack the element of adoration and oblation through which the wearisome task of co-operating with life is transfigured and made intelligible?"[60] De la Perraudière reflected on the prospect of death in a letter to a friend who was a member of a different religious order. He wrote: "That which struck me . . . is how much we others, religious, we can regard death with simplicity, as an accident more or less sudden, but predicted; how much each holds on a little to a place in the world, and how beautiful it is to be able to leave to find God without the ties that hold you here, and to leave the earth, not like a stone that one seizes with great struggle from a cavity made for it, but rather like a stone which becomes free immediately, rejoined to its center of gravity."[61]

Seminarian Lavergne, by then a corporal, in his last letter to his director from the battlefield near Arras compared the act of dying in battle to the sacrifice priests offer on the altar. He wrote on September 5, 1915:

To die for the country, on hill 123 or on hill 140, is a fate certainly very enviable for one who dreams of the priesthood, for there is in the sacrifice of life, prematurely accomplished for a just cause, many of the elements of sacerdotal immolation. I always remember this phrase that they read to us in our spiritual readings, in the work of R. P. Perroy, when I was studying philosophy at the minor seminary: "To die on the cross, that is to say in total abandonment and, if God permits, with a taste of bile on one's lips, oh precious death in the eyes of the

Savior!" . . . One dies a little like that around hill 123, I have realized this in the nights I have spent burying the desiccated, massacred, and abandoned bodies.[62]

The priests' descriptions of their experiences and feelings during the war wavered continuously between patriotism and love for the front on the one hand, and horror at war on the other. They demonstrate that in the crucible of the war, priests endured a moral struggle, which helped them connect with their own humanity and with their bonds to their countrymen and to their country. It earned for them a new respect from their colleagues and from the country at large, and at the same time they came to feel a bond with their fellow countrymen, regardless of their religiosity.

There is indeed much similarity between the feelings of national sentiment among the soldiers, described by the historian Stéphane Audoin-Rouzeau, and those of the priests. Audoin-Rouzeau portrays the soldiers as not enthusiastic for the war, but determined to fulfill their duty. They were convinced of the justice of the French cause and the need to defend their country from invasion and to protect the sacred graves of the dead. These sentiments he believes tied them to the national community and secured their identity. Although the priests found a religious significance in the sacrifices of war, which many of their fellow soldiers did not, their experiences and their actions proclaimed their solidarity with their comrades in arms and with the national community, a solidarity that had been perceived to have been broken before the war.[63]

In this novel situation, the priests, whether noncombatant or combatant, also managed to reprise and adapt their more traditional roles as comforters and consolers of their fellow soldiers. Their participation in the war provided the basis for a newfound acceptance among men, who for years had been absent from their churches. Their work on developing these new relationships will be explored in the next chapter.

CHAPTER FIVE

PRIESTS AS MILITARY PASTORS

Wartime Adaptations of Traditional Roles

In the maelstrom of war, priests found themselves more valued as pastors than they had been for more than forty years. Concerned for years with the absence of men in the churches, they were thrilled to have so many men to serve. No longer were they isolated in "a sacristy between darkened chandeliers," but rather they were in bustling wartime posts, serving soldiers and civilians in the most dire circumstances. They were active in the trenches, on the battlefront, and in towns devoid of churches and pastors. They put in long hours responding to distraught relatives begging for information on missing or dead soldiers.

They took care to look after the soldiers' temporal needs, soliciting money and treats for the soldiers from organizations created to help with the war effort and from their own family members. They helped soldiers communicate with their families, took on the responsibility of informing relatives of the plight of their soldiers, saw to finding and identifying bodies, burying the dead, and marking the graves. They also acted as intermediaries with military authority, seeking to mitigate punishment for soldiers who had disobeyed orders. In their communications to the press and to friends and superiors, they praised the soldiers and described their hardships. Slowly, as they interacted with the soldiers, feelings of comradeship grew apace with a new confidence in their acceptance as pastors.

Priests understood that the soldiers they joined at the beginning of the war had had little contact with the clergy in their former lives. Not only chaplains but also other noncombatants, stretcher-bearers, and nurses sought to win the trust of the men by providing for their material needs. In August 1914 Achille Liénart joined the troops as unofficial chaplain as they took up quarters at Thenaille in Picardy. He felt he had the opportunity to "completely win over the hearts of my soldiers, by profiting from the freedom I enjoyed, to go each day on foot to Vervins to buy them the things they needed." He saw the results immediately because, despite his unofficial status, and realizing his situation, a sergeant and a corporal invited him to eat with their squad. He said that this gesture made him feel "adopted" by the soldiers.[1]

Priests described providing such services throughout the war in numerous letters and memoirs. Stretcher-bearer Teilhard de Chardin asked his cousin to send "woolies" and a "football" in February 1915 when he was serving in Picardy. Concerned for the comfort and amusement of his fellow soldiers, he wrote: "What the men lack most of all, even more than warm clothing is some means of distraction, games and books. There are great drawbacks to cards, and they're not very desirable. Perhaps some small draught-boards (cardboard) or something of that sort would do as well. Books (historical stories or novels, paper-backed) would be eagerly competed for."[2] Abbé Georges Ardant recounted that when the troops were preparing for the battle of Verdun in the fall of 1916, he took commissions from soldiers to buy things, to pick up mail, and to send mail to their families.[3]

Chaplains also tried to give soldiers as much of a respite from the war as possible by creating spaces with a homey feeling whenever they could. Abbé Liénart described his efforts during November 1915 in the trenches of Sapigneul in the Marne area where the troops spent the winter. He explained: "In Grandes Places, I am busy building a little rudimentary shelter which will serve as a chapel and reading room for the soldiers. During the day, a curtain separates the altar where the Blessed Sacrament will be placed, and the soldiers will be able to come into the room freely. It will be the only shelter in the camp in which they will be able to stand up at full height, because all the others are built under an inclined roof which descends to the ground like the canvas of a tent."[4] The soldiers confided in him during these rest periods, reading him their letters from home and entrusting him with letters for their family.[5]

Chaplain Paul Doncoeur took great pleasure in visiting the soldiers on the front line or in their trenches. He brought them news of the sector and cigarettes, at the same time as he offered his priestly services of confession or communion to those who wanted them. When they were in the rear, after evening prayers, five or ten camarades, especially the young ones, often came to his shelter for a "grog of friendship." His biographer attests that Doncoeur, who was just fifteen years older than most of the soldiers, relished the daily contact with these young men, an experience he had never had, since he was separated from them by his exile as a young Jesuit. He felt strongly all that he had missed of youthful companionship. The young men, too, appreciated his kindness and his attention to all the details of their lives. For them he was "the father in the middle of his children."[6]

When he received a new assignment in March 1915, Abbé Liénart wrote that he felt "truly heartbroken to be separated from the men whose lives, anxieties, and sufferings he had shared intimately." He continued: "On this occasion I received from them the most moving expressions of this virile friendship."[7] When he was reassigned, he got his request, to be with a regiment from his own region, the Nord, the 201st Infantry. The only priest they had had was a soldier priest, who was recently killed. He was determined to live with the soldiers rather than the officers. He rejoiced: "I had now as a 'military parish' a combat infantry unit whose risks, sufferings, and glories I was going to share, and where I was going to exercise, among the living and the dying, a sacerdotal ministry which would make its imprint on my whole life and would leave me with the most moving memories."[8]

Volunteer chaplain Louis Lenoir relished his wartime pastoral duties. He felt he was very much needed and wanted. He described for a friend a typical day in the chaos of war, between November 10 and December 21, 1914:

> In the morning, mass with a sermon in a barn, for the battalions who are in the sheltered trenches. . . . Always very many communions, sometimes three and four hundred. Then I go to the firing line of hill 191. I slip from one communicating trench to another, from one battlement to the next, from one brazier to another, chatting, joking, preaching, absolving, giving communion, writing letters, drying tears, distributing gifts as I can with my scandalous salary, and often, alas! collecting the wounded or the dying. . . . It is sufficient for the chaplain to come to them and shake their hands to win them over. . . . All are happy nevertheless to see the cassock near them; very many profit from it. Either it is a prodigal who wants to confess and become a child of God again; or a brave one who is leaving on patrol, and wishes first to fortify himself by receiving communion.[9]

Assigned to the troops in the Forest of Parroy in the spring of 1916, the chaplain, Abbé Lagardère, wrote: "Here I am curé of a parish of three thousand souls." He fulfilled his duties with enthusiasm, evangelizing both civilian parishioners and soldiers, catechizing, and visiting the sick. He went by bicycle to the surrounding villages and to the trenches.[10] Other chaplains wrote of serving both the communes neighboring the battlefields as well as the troops, saying masses, even serving as the priest for first communions and baptisms to many parishes that were missing pastors because of the war.

In the trenches and on the battlefield, soldiers turned for pastoral care not only to chaplains but also to priests and seminarians who were combatants. The seminarian Bernard Lavergne described his new relationship with his men in his role as their corporal. He wrote to his family from Berry au Bac in the fall of 1914 that the twelve men in his squad had become like a family and he served as both father and mother. They came to him when things did not function well. He described himself as the one who "leads them through the maze of communication trenches to the post that they must occupy before the enemy . . . to whom they admit their fatigue and confide their boredom . . . who is concerned to give them time to rest, to wash and to find water."[11]

Similarly, the twenty-year-old seminarian Jean Nourisson wrote to a friend from Rouen on August 26, 1914, that despite the physical hardships, his life was rather "sweet." He found sympathy among his fellow soldiers. They questioned him about his métier and he felt that he was dispelling prejudice against priests by his interaction. He wrote again on September 10, 1914, that the men confided in him stories of their family and of their work, of how they lost their faith, and he could explain to them the celibate life of a priest, and the social morality of the Church in these conversations.[12]

Occasionally, because they were known to be priests, combatants would be asked to serve in traditional priestly roles, even if it took them away from their ordinary responsibilities. Jean Julien Weber, who was a captain, not a chaplain, described one such occasion. General de Bouillon asked Weber to accompany a bereaved colonel to the funeral of his eighteen-year-old son. Weber said that he agreed to go on this errand of mercy, although he felt he should remain with his regiment.[13]

Léonce Raffin, the forty-one-year-old stretcher-bearer who was also serving as an unofficial chaplain to an artillery group in 1916, described another kind of counseling which undoubtedly took place often. He recounted that while they were serving in the area of the Somme, a young *maréchal des logis* approached him in great anxiety. He confided that he had received an anonymous letter that claimed he was not the father of his wife's new baby. Raffin suspected the report's veracity and began asking questions about the man's wife, whether he had written to her, whether she lived near her parents, whether she was religious. All the answers were yes. He told him to go home and everything would be fine. When Raffin next met the maréchal he learned that his suspicions were well founded. The anonymous letter came from a nursemaid the maréchal's wife had dismissed. Raffin commented: "No one knows how much moral suffering occurred at the front, which was confided to the priest! And sometimes so many worries were without foundation, alas!"[14]

Chaplains were authorized by military authority to dedicate themselves to their pastoral role, providing spiritual comfort and support. Unlike the stretcher-bearers and combatants, they had no other official duties. Thirty-nine-year-old Charles Thellier de Poncheville, who served as official chaplain with the troops in the area of Verdun for ten months, described how much the soldiers depended on him for comfort, when he visited them in their trenches before a battle or as they lay dying. He wrote of going to some men in a ravine, who were "susceptible to a friendly visit. No one is concerned what others think of him in approaching the priest. Suffering and death have accomplished here a profound rapprochement. We chat in small groups, randomly as I go by, in an intimacy I have never known before."[15] He also believed that the masses he said on Sundays gave the troops a sense of normalcy, reminding them of family and home.

When Chaplain Jean Lagardère learned that the wounded could not be transported from the battlefields of Champagne, he engaged two soldiers to accompany him to the front line at one in the morning. Under heavy shelling, it took them two hours to reach it. He described the scene: "There I am. I place myself at the front of the aide post where the most severely wounded were brought. I minister to them and hear confessions. . . . I am going to see the battlefield. Dead everywhere . . . the image of the inferno, some wounded . . . others buried: I disengage one here, another there. I return to the aide post and I begin my work: they identify the bodies and then the last of the wounded is taken away."[16] Lagardère met his own death on November 4, 1918, at the age of fifty-eight, serving his men on the battlefield.[17]

Writing back to his newspaper, *La Croix de Cantal*, volunteer chaplain, Abbé Marcelin Lissorgues described "the incredible cruelty" of the war that he witnessed among the dead and dying on the battlefields of Verdun in the summer of 1917. He cursed those responsible for the "appalling catastrophe" as he strove to serve.[18] He explained:

> The anguish of the chaplain is to not be sufficient to his task, during the days and nights of the battle. How can he be able to tear himself away from the cot of a wounded man whose rough hand clutches his with all the force of a poor life that is slipping away? Moreover from all the stretchers lined up in the night, pleas and calls emerge. "Chaplain! Chaplain!" All want to see him bending above them in their misery. They wait for him to give them, besides religious help for which I have found them eager, the truth about their condition. They charge him with intimate missions. They speak to him of their home, of their "wife,"— "the poor thing, she has worked so much!"—of their children who are truly good little ones. . . . Ah! The depressing hours! I escaped for several minutes, to a darker corner of the sap, to weep.[19]

In describing his ordinary duties, Lissorgues, who served from December 1916 until March 1919, placed a great deal of emphasis on helping soldiers to remain rooted in their families as a source of stability and normalcy. He wrote: "The chaplain must lend a patient ear to the poilu who never tires of speaking of his family, of his little ones who are notably, ordinarily prodigies. One must listen with interest to the reading of innumerable, crumpled letters drawn from deep pockets. One must help the poilu, who is less educated, with his correspondence and not recoil before the task of writing a kind letter to some sweet fiancée."[20] Other chaplains told of using their leaves to visit families and bring letters from the soldiers and gifts in return. One of these, Pierre Lelièvre, a volunteer chaplain, visited soldiers' relatives in Brittany, at their request, before an anticipated offensive.[21]

Priests also often took up the sad responsibility, sometimes confided by the soldiers, and sometimes on their own initiative, to contact the families of men who had been wounded or killed. Liénart wrote that during the Battle of the Somme, he was given letters from the soldiers to send to their families if the worst befell them: "Indeed I spent the morning in the empty road hearing the confessions and giving communion. When I finished my soldiers gave me their letters, for very many, perhaps their last. They have written however they are able, in pencil, on their knees, before combat. . . . I have carried as many as 300 of them to the aide post of Hardecourt. I have done well to remain and to walk among my dear soldiers, my head wrapped warmly under my helmet."[22]

Some families sought information from chaplains when they did not receive any communication from their relatives. In the archival files of the Bureau of Volunteer Chaplains there are letters asking for help from chaplains in finding out the plight of relatives and friends. A letter from a father in Paris dated December 8, 1914, stated: "Having heard that the Office of Military Chaplains has the goodness to concern itself with soldiers who have disappeared, I would be very appreciative if you take into consideration my request concerning my son, the soldier Louis Etienne Marcel Lechaudel of the 168th Infantry Regiment, 4th Company of Toul . . . wounded in combat on September 11 . . . and disappeared since then, no news has reached us since." A follow-up letter was attached dated December 15, thanking the office for finding the location of his son.[23]

In another poignant communication a relative wrote in 1914: "They tell me that you have a list of several chaplains of regiments and I appeal to your great charity; since the 18th of August we have had no news of my nephew, Pierre de Vallais, sergeant in the 79th Infantry of Nancy." The writer asks for the name of the chaplain of this regiment and states: "Perhaps the chaplain knows something about this subject." And another writes on behalf of an ailing mother on December 11, 1914: "I have the honor of coming to ask of your compassionate heart, some news for a poor mother, whose son has been fighting from the beginning of the war, a member of the class of 1913, and from whom this dear *Maman* has not received news since the first of November." The communication, addressed to an unnamed priest, begged for news, and described a mother in failing health and an honest boy who is devout. The letter provided information regarding the company and the regiment.[24]

These letters to the Bureau of Volunteer Chaplains continued throughout the war. Sometimes a chaplain might be the only recourse for information because so many officers were killed in the battles. A letter dated May 21, 1915, from an aunt described one such situation:

We do not have the precise details of the last days before the glorious death of our dear child, and up until now have not been enlightened: all the officers having, alas, been killed the same day in the same engagement. We learned only recently, a soldier of the regiment assured us, that a chaplain was attached to the 279th Infantry on that date in August—. Would it be possible, sir, to verify that assertion from the list of chaplains; and to let us know who that chaplain is, and if he is still with the 279th? The regiment has been reformed, because it has suffered losses so, whom shall we address? It is a heart-rending anguish you understand![25]

After the war Grandmaison and Veuillot attempted to evaluate the work of the chaplains whom the Bureau of Volunteer Chaplains had placed in the battlefield. They stated that the correspondence with families was perhaps the most "intimate" and at the same time the most "influential" part of their work. It absorbed a great deal of the chaplains' time. Abbé Charles Umbricht wrote to the Bureau, apologizing for the long time that had passed since he had written. He said that his days were consumed visiting the trenches and his nights were occupied with responding to ten, fifteen, and sometimes twenty letters from families asking for information.[26]

The Bureau believed that this correspondence helped the priests to accomplish much good and gave them important contacts in working sensitively with the men and their families. They quote the Capuchin chaplain Father Paul-Albert Fardet, who wrote: "Ah! These letters of the Chaplain to mothers, spouses, they always cost me. To inform them of a severe wound, but to leave some hope, to give vague details about the death, the reality of which, if known would rack them with tears! Sublime and holy mission of the priest who, while opening their hearts to deep wounds, must comfort them with words from Scripture which will soothe and bring strength to their sacrifice!"[27]

Flagéat also found multiple stacks of priests' letters in the Jesuit archives written in response to mothers who wanted information on sons who had disappeared, or to those who asked that a cross be placed on the tomb of their sons, but did not know where they were buried. There are letters to parents who want to know the last words their sons said as they were dying in the chaplain's arms. All inquiries were assiduously and carefully answered to the best of the ability of the chaplains.[28]

A number of priests describe consoling men waiting to be judged for self-mutilation or for refusing to fight. Jean Lagardère recounted counseling a twenty-year-old young cyclist who was guilty of mutilating his right hand:

While waiting for judgment, I approach this tall child of twenty. I take him by the hand, and with maternal tenderness I scold him gently and ask him to open his soul to me, for the present hour could be his last. He becomes like a little child, he expresses good feelings . . . no more evil than any other by nature, but he does not know how to obey, he is undisciplined, he had some bad reports and no sympathy. I scrape away the dross that covers his existence, and go back without effort to his first communion. There, I find the pious child who knows how to believe, who knows how to pray and who knows how to love. . . . He confesses, he repents, he is moved. . . . We recite the rosary together. The minutes go by. I go and ask for the verdict: he is condemned to five years in prison.

Lagardère said that the staff officers were not happy with the light sentence, but he took the opportunity to complain that the military high command wanted young soldiers to be heroes, but did not understand how important it was for these young men who were away from the guidance of their families to have access to a priest.[29]

Chaplains were often asked to minister to those soldiers who were condemned to death, and sometimes the priests' pleas for pardon were heard. In one instance quoted by Grandmaison and Veuillot, Father Fardet, chaplain during the Battle of the Dardanelles, was able to win pardon for several men as they were standing before the firing squad. He wrote that he pleaded pardon on condition that they would return immediately to the front line. At first, he said the captain seemed inflexible, but he continued with his plea and was ultimately successful.[30]

An incident recorded by Abbé Georges Ardant before the battle of Verdun indicates that priests did not always win such a happy result. On October 20, 1916, he learned that the War Council had condemned two soldiers to death. The execution was to be early the next morning at 6:30 A.M. He and his colleague, Abbé Louis Castelin, wanted to try an approach to the commander, General Maurice Sarrail. The head doctor loaned them a car and they set out at night for Verdun. Several officers encouraged them to try. They had difficulty finding the general's headquarters, however, and never reached it in time to save the two soldiers.[31]

As they served with the soldiers, the priests found much to admire. They felt it was their duty to describe the bravery and perseverance of the poilu to the press and friends and superiors on the home front. From his earliest experiences, Abbé Lelièvre, who is much praised by postwar antiwar authors for his expressions of disapproval for the war, admired the bravery and resilience of the French soldier. He wrote in his war journal on September 14, 1914, as the troops were in retreat: "Whether he is resting, marching or fighting, he has an unbelievable initiative, is always gay, smiling, singing, a tiny bit cheeky, is also as tough as any soldier in the world. In this retreat without end, no one complains of fatigue, but always of moving back." He did not have the same praise for the officers, who he claimed were: "Nervous, irritable, domineering, making it very apparent that they were not made to exercise the authority they possess. . . . Thus it is the general complaint of the soldiers that they are commanded badly. How many incomprehensible orders, badly interpreted, with impossible execution, cancelled."[32]

The thirty-four-year-old Jesuit Lt. Paul Dubrulle was full of praise for his men who took part in the Battle of Verdun. He was ordained a priest on August 2, 1914, the day mobilization was decreed. He was promoted to second lieutenant after the Battle of the Somme. He wrote of his regiment that they were continuously bombarded and had to take a very difficult hill, *la croupe d'Haudromont*. After describing one of the assaults he wrote: "The spectacle was beautiful, but what was beautiful above all, was the attitude of the men. . . . They found themselves at the most critical hour faced by a strong and confident enemy, powerfully equipped, and they remained completely calm. I saw them fire, with assurance, a bit swiftly, without doubt, but without haste. They talked among themselves, passing useful information, even joking. One would think this was an exercise, except for this noble elevation of the soul that one only rediscovers under fire."[33]

Official chaplain Thellier de Poncheville, criticized for his unthinking patriotism by postwar antiwar authors, nonetheless wrote that civilians should come to Verdun if they wanted to understand the reality of war. He asked himself why the soldiers persevered in the face of such destruction. He had his own regiment wiped out. He wrote in praise of the soldiers:

The mission that these men have received is to be crushed in place. They [their superiors] will put others in their place when they will be no more. They will not even pick them up to bury them; pushed into the soil under monstrous battering blows, they will continue to fight to their last breath, as they have fought to the last drop of blood. . . . Why are they [the soldiers] there? For what irresistible reasons does their country abandon them to this carnage? They do not know perhaps. But the strict and formidable duty of the present hour, they know well: it is to hold to the last. And all do their duty . . . they have confidence in each other. By their feeling of solidarity, by self-esteem, by fraternal and natural courage, no one will betray his companions. A person is strong when suffering with everyone else. One link at a time, they forge the chain which will not break.[34]

Chaplain Marcelin Lissorgues, as director of *La Croix du Cantal*, published much of his journal in its pages. He claimed his purpose was to recount the truth about the war and the soldiers to people on the home front. With the troops in Argonne, on March 18, 1917, he wrote to dispel the idea promulgated in some newspapers that the troops were having a good time. He explained: "On the faith of the narrators who describe the front without leaving the boulevard, one can believe that no Frenchman is more jovial than the man in the trenches, and that the camps littered with shriveled straw were resounding with jokes and endless laughter. These pictures are absurd and irritating."[35]

Lissorgues had written earlier, on March 11, to contradict reports from the home front that the troops were ready to give up fighting: "I heard it said once, in the interior, that the men on the front 'have had enough' and that if the war did not come to an end quickly enough, they would refuse to fight for a long time." He emphasized that the soldiers were not willing to accept defeat:

I have not heard a single soldier who accepts the idea of defeat. The poilus aspire to peace with enthusiastic ardor. They take pleasure in the hope that it will be very soon. Certain ones, at the end of each month, are profoundly astonished that the armistice has not yet occurred. They appear surprised that Germany is so strong. But the idea that France could be conquered never occurs to them, and there, without doubt, is a magnificent state of mind.[36]

It was not only the bravery of the soldiers that the priests described. Albert Bessières, a thirty-seven-year-old stretcher-bearer, commented on those men who served as porters and as workers digging trenches and building fortifications, who served for hours in muddy trenches "without measure, without profit, without glory. And I see that no glory is equal to that of being one of them. . . . A superhuman patience is affirmed, even amidst cries of revolt, and in spite of the drinking bouts and binges, the cursing, proclaiming the depth of Christianity which was imparted to them and which survived. . . . Then, they partake of the eternal blessing: 'Blessed are the poor!'"[37]

The priests' admiration for the soldiers grew despite their realization that many of the soldiers would never embrace religion. Chaplain Lelièvre already understood this fact in the late fall of 1914 when the troops were at rest: "At Simencourt, our chats became lively discussions, and I affirm that no one avoided them. Not that I have a great hope of changing whatever is the state of their souls . . . but I firmly believe it is good that they remember a priest who questions himself as much as they do, and more, and whose sincerity will appear to them, I hope, unquestionable." But he lamented: "But great God! Why such an incomplete formation of their Christian souls! So many of them discarded the faith only because it came from an authority figure. They have a horror of believing just because the Church teaches it." He blamed their professors at the Catholic schools they attended for not providing arguments to support their faith when first confronting what he deemed the "intoxication with science."[38]

Occasions for such conversations are mentioned in priests' letters and memoirs frequently. One can hazard a guess that there were many more than are described. Teilhard de Chardin recounted one such conversation in the citadel of Verdun on November 6, 1918:

> I was having a comfortable glass of beer with a lieutenant who is a friend of mine. . . . Our conversation gradually turned to moral life; and then I saw that my companion was a fervent disciple of the 'religion of the spirit.' His attitude is this: he believes in our Lord, he reads the Gospels constantly, he offers up to God all his actions as so many prayers . . . but he wants no dogma, no ritual, no 'organized religion.' He's above all that. . . . I tried, without much success, to show him how contradictory his attitude was.[39]

While some of the chaplains lamented the behavior of soldiers during rest periods away from the front, priests who were commanders tried hard to understand them and even to defend them. The Jesuit officer Frédéric de Bélinay defended the behavior of his troops in a letter to a fellow Jesuit,

Claude Chanteur, on November 22, 1914: "I hear neither blasphemies nor curses. I see no immorality. If sometimes the men, exhausted with weariness, coming back to the trenches at seven in the evening, snatch a chicken or a bottle of wine from the owner of an abandoned house, it seems to me that one must excuse them, since their dinner will not be cooked before two in the morning, and the water is sure to give us typhoid." Flagéat claimed that Jesuits usually tried to empathize with the men who surrounded them, as Bélinay did. They sought to overlook appearances because they felt that the feelings and motivations of the soldiers were most often laudable.[40]

Lt. Jean Julien Weber was also more tolerant than many of his colleagues of the men at rest, where, he said, they had more distractions like open-air cinema, phonographs, and theater. He wrote: "A little more immorality among the officers, due to the organization of vice (at Châlons, and in all the cities in the rear) and the long duration of the war. They want to compensate for their boredom, to 'kill le cafard' sometimes."[41]

In his later memoir Weber explained that he found it necessary to learn to command with humanity and understanding. He felt that the successful leader had to temper discipline with kindness and compassion. He wrote: "You realize—and I understood this especially when I was made Captain, in 1916—that you bear responsibility for the life of your companions in battle and that you do not have the right to dispose of it carelessly or recklessly."[42] After the offensive in Champagne, he was concerned with the "mentality" of the men. He identified some common traits: "a little weariness, some grumbling, but they march in spite of everything. There is not too much enthusiasm, except when it is time to fight, but a somewhat fatalist resignation. Some very beautiful souls, a few rascals, and very much moral mediocrity: the same as in civilian life. 'It is easier to die well than to live well,' as my former professor, M. de La Serre wrote me."[43]

Captain Weber even sympathized with men who mutinied in 1917. His comments, of course, might have been influenced by the fact that he put his notebooks together in periods of convalescence during the war, but published them much later. He condemned Nivelle's Chemin-des-Dames campaign, stating that he had refused to heed warnings of some subordinates, and observed: "The 16th of April is a fateful date for very many poilus and for the morale of all." His regiment was not involved in the attack because it was busy with construction projects in the area of Dannemarie. His opinion of the outcome, expressed in his war journal, was nuanced: "While Nivelle is replaced by [General Philippe] Pétain on May 15th, discontent still grows among the troops, and soon there are serious mutinies. The High Command manages the crisis smoothly and finally averts it with a minimum of severity: out of the 412 death sentences pronounced by the war councils between May and October, only fifty-five men were executed (eight of them for crimes of common law)."[44] From then on, the High Command was generally more concerned with improving the daily lives of the soldiers. In addition, they attempted to organize the trains more efficiently so that men going on leave might reach home before their leave expired. They encouraged officers to be "more human" with the poilus and to get closer to them. Hoping to prevent further demonstrations, they furnished colonels with a monthly account of troop morale and sent officers extracts of soldiers' letters gathered by the censors. He concluded that the demonstrations were also a good thing because they revealed the intolerable maneuvers the men were obliged to make and exposed the bad preparation for offensives.[45]

The sympathy and admiration the priests felt for the troops is most dramatically portrayed in Jesuit chaplain Georges Guitton's book, *Avec un régiment de l'Armée Gouraud le 415e d'infanterie: La poursuite victorieuse, 26 septembre–11 novembre 1918*. Instead of writing a personal memoir of his service, he described the battles and brave exploits of the unit he accompanied. To assure its accuracy and to give voice to the soldiers, he carefully solicited their comments and remembrances. Unlike other priests, he mentioned few masses or confessions and did not describe the religious feelings of the soldiers.[46]

From the outset, priests were very concerned with providing proper burial for the dead. Chaplain Jean Lagardère, called the burial of the dead a sacred duty. He wrote: "That is the task of the apostle, it is the forced march of the good pastor; it is the painful debt to pay to duty, to give an example, to perform a sacred work, however repugnant, and to save souls."[47] This did not just concern chaplains, however. The Jesuit commander Bélinay wrote of getting volunteers to bury the dead on the night of November 2 and 3, 1914: "I asked for a group to be assigned to bury the dead, which were in a pile of beetroots. Our doctor Sasportés, a man of incomparable devotion, followed me. It was not a trivial thing to go and wake up ten cavalrymen: they slept buried under a pile of straw. I led them to the place. Our dead were indeed there. Their comrades, whom I had spoken of, had not been touched."[48]

From the beginning of the war, Abbé Liénart was concerned with burying the dead, making sure that there were crosses on graves and making careful maps of burial sites so that he could inform families. In the battlefield of Verdun, despite beginning to feel feverish, he felt he had to fulfill this last duty before seeking treatment: "Our dead remained on the ground, summarily buried in a shell hole behind our trenches. We had not been able to place crosses with their names during the battle. I made the list, I noted the locations. I had poor crosses made and engraved with names, and I sought some men of good will who would return to help me to fulfill this pious duty."[49] Later on the Somme, in September 1916, he explained that after a battle he immediately went to look for the dead and the disappeared. He wrote: "I found a number of them, but not all. The bodies of lieutenant de Saint Jean and second lieutenant Bockstael have disappeared. My exploration was suddenly interrupted by a rain of shells which fell on us and obliged us to go to ground in a trench."[50]

In 1918, Liénart was able to entirely remake the cemetery of Blanc-Sablon, near the Chemin des Dames, thanks to the plan of burials he made immediately after the attack. They had gathered the bodies in a shell hole, with their names in bottles, because there was no time for a proper burial. With the help of a group of musicians, they returned four times to bury the dead and place crosses on their graves. The site had been ravaged in later attacks, but they managed to discover other bodies they had missed the year before.[51]

Georges Ardant, the forty-eight-year-old volunteer chaplain, described recruiting the priest from the little parish nearby, as well as the chaplain of the military hospital and an officer, to photograph the graves where the "heroes of Éparges" rested after their battle in April 1915. He subsequently sent the photographs to their families, who had sent requests to have commemorative plaques placed on the graves.[52]

Military authorities often expressed a great deal of appreciation for the activity of priests on the battlefield. During the course of his duties as chaplain, Liénart was cited for bravery in going to the front line in the most difficult circumstances, caring for the wounded, and burying the dead without regard to his own safety. He mentioned the citations in his journal, claiming it was most important to him that his first citation was written by his colonel, Hebmann, who was a Protestant, recognizing his continued service from 1914 through June 1915. Later when he received the Croix de Guerre decorated with a bronze star, he was especially pleased to receive encouraging words from the general for his service in the "inferno of Verdun" in 1916. He claimed to be even more moved by the cordial compliments of his soldiers.[53]

Franciscan Édouard de Massat was cited in the order of the day on June 8, 1915, for his work in burying the dead. The citation stated: "He took the initiative to organize a team of volunteers, who for fifteen days, exhumed the bodies of Zouaves, who had fallen in combat in September and had been hastily buried by the enemy, in order to identify them and give them a suitable burial."[54]

The affirmation the soldiers gave the priests was more important to them than all the accolades and citations they received from military authorities. They were encouraged by demonstrations of affection to believe that their work was appreciated. One of the most interesting expressions of this affection was expressed in sonnet form for Chaplain Jean Lagardère, after he received a citation for going night and day to the trenches to attend to the dying in August 1917. He was one of the most notorious chaplains, renowned for standing up for his convictions in discussions about religious matters and even for fighting back when someone just wanted to pick a fight. Officers recalled his "holy fits of anger" and "outbursts of piety and faith." Nonetheless, the men esteemed and loved him as these verses attest:

> When you come in the evening, our shelter lights up.
> . . . .
> You unite our hearts in an extraordinary accord.
> Death seems easy to us in that instant,
> Because it would be blessed by your hand.
> If there is a peaceful hearth so very near the enemy
> Which unites us here in serving the Patrie,
> You are the father there and the priest and the friend.[55]

Lelièvre's soldiers also demonstrated their appreciation for him in verse with a song they composed in May 1916. He had served months with them in the sector of Ecurie-Roclincourt, the most active and difficult area during the advance on Arras, when they surprised him with this song at the evening gathering just before the battle. The song, "La chanson du Curé de Roclinque," played on the place name of the sector. The lyrics described a vicar from Ménilmontant who goes to the front. One verse stated:

He wears a cap on his head
And tucking up his cassock
He follows with nerve
On his bicycle,
Hearing confessions under machine-gun fire

The last verse stated:

Taking part in the battle,
He had more work really
Than in Ménilmont
We hope moreover
That he will think from time to time
Of his buddies in the regiment
At Ménilmontant[56]

André Ducasse described the reaction of soldiers who were not particularly religious to the role of priests on the battlefield. He gathered testimony from rank and file soldiers for his book, *La guerre racontée par les combattants: Anthologie des écrivains du front*. He intended to provide a true description of the war of 1914–18, not based on official accounts, on the memoirs of generals, or on the work of *romanciers*, who portrayed the war melodramatically. A long quotation from a memoir by Georges Gaudy, who fought at Verdun, dated May 15, 1916, dramatically portrays the profound impact of a chaplain's service on the soldiers:

I went to wander in the courtyards of the fort full of accumulated debris, of foul waste. I saw a priest with a helmet who was hurrying by and followed by several poilus. I joined them without knowing what they were going to do. The expression on this chaplain's face struck me, sad features which seemed to express all the human suffering, but which was allayed by a veil of inexpressible kindness and resignation. . . .

We went into a subterranean cave, close and empty. The priest took from his chest a little crucifix. He fixed it on the wall and, remaining immobile before it, he extended his arms in a cross and for a long time I saw him, his regard directed towards the victim. . . . What was he doing? His lips were not moving. The meditation was all interior and the face became still more sad. . . . My companions, standing along the wall, remained silent. Some had their arms crossed, eyes on the ground; others held themselves very straight, with their helmets in their hands. I studied their faces, strong with rough beards, their looks empty or feverish, their posture bent like old men with inconceivable fatigue. They were not speaking; they were not praying. What were they thinking? What were they believing? . . .

The priest turned around slowly; he looked at us one after the other, walking slowly around the gloomy group with eyes which seemed to want to cry. And then he spoke of trembling hopes, saying it was necessary to accomplish the tasks of each day, not to think too much about the future, that thought of future sufferings would be an intolerable burden . . . and the poilus listened, heads bent, understanding that the era of martyrdom was not ended, that they would have still to march, to suffer, to bleed.[57]

Ducasse confirms the impressions of priests and other witnesses that the priests did indeed have a profound impact on the soldiers. He wrote: "Living very near the men (who never would confide entirely in an officer or a stranger) they knew them better and would never betray them; they were moved with compassion."[58]

One of the most important services the priest performed on the battlefield was to provide for masses and other ceremonies to honor the soldiers' fallen comrades. Chaplains routinely said memorial masses for the dead and spoke at many funerals, using the occasions to both honor the dead and encourage and console the bereaved soldiers. In the area of Verdun on March 23, 1916, Thellier de Poncheville recounted that a group of survivors brought back one of their comrades for a Requiem mass: "Oppressed by visions of the drama which they left behind, all breathless with these very strong emotions, they are eager to hear the words of pity and hope that the priest offers them in the name of God."[59]

Recognizing the importance of these masses to the troops, chaplains tried to provide them regardless of the difficulties posed by the battle. Liénart described a scene in the midst of the Battle of the Somme. Although the 201st had captured a German battery, they had lost 44 officers and 168 men and were badly in need of reinforcements. He wrote: "We were hardly able on September 11 to sing an outdoor Requiem mass in the woods of Célestins for our dead of the 4th and 6th battalions before we had to leave in time to prepare another mass at Sailly-Laurette for the 5th battalion."[60]

Chaplains took advantage of periods of rest to organize memorials for the dead and to render homage to those who had disappeared. In fact, Louis Lenoir instituted a month of Requiem masses for those killed in different companies. Many inquiries from families also demonstrated that these masses were a consolation to families as well as to the soldiers.[61]

Requiem masses drew more participants than Sunday masses, according to many witnesses. Annette Becker found documentation for this observation in photographs of masses at the front, and hypothesized that the soldiers' attendance at services for their fallen companions was more an expression of comradely homage, a way of continuing to live together for a few more minutes, than an act of faith.[62] Nonetheless, their presence at the masses demonstrated that the soldiers and their families found comfort in the priests' service and valued it.

During the war, then, priests had quickly adapted their traditional roles as pastors to the battlefield. A number of them used the term "parish" to describe their responsibilities on the battlefield or in the hospitals. They speedily realized the way to care for their parishioners and build up trust. They were thrilled to be serving parishes filled with men who had been absent from their churches prior to the war. They did not balk at the extraordinarily difficult measures that were necessary in order to "serve" their parishes, traveling by bicycle, horse, and car or on foot, sloshing through mud, braving shellfire. They sought to create a feeling of home not only through the means of masses and religious services, but by providing shelters where men could congregate, read, or play games.

Remarkably, considering the de-Christianization that had progressed during the nineteenth century, the men responded, assuming the role of parishioners. Not only did they accept priestly services, they sought them, especially when wounded or dying, but even when just troubled by news from home. The priests served as an important means of communicating with families. They took care to respect the bodies of the fallen soldiers and provide burials and markers on graves. They provided memorial services for the dead close to the battlefields, which witnesses attest were the most well attended of Catholic services. The comfort of the priests' presence was universally remarked.

The priests' role in the war was based on their profound desire to be of service to their fellow soldiers and to their country. They had willingly and astonishingly participated as warriors, joined in the fervor of battle even when they had been assigned other roles, and generously shared the horrors of the battlefield and the miseries of the trenches. They slowly modified their aspirations to be missionaries on the battlefield to adapting traditional pastoral roles to the needs of the soldiers. They served at times as confidants and consolers, and at others provided material comforts and reminders of home. They helped soldiers and military authorities to communicate with families of the wounded and the dead. Most importantly to the bereaved comrades and families, they took care to assure proper burial and services for the dead. In the next chapter we will explore whether the roles they had assumed during the war changed their postwar relationships with their countrymen and with their government.

CHAPTER SIX

MEMORY OF WAR IN POSTWAR RELATIONS

The French priests' experience reflects the truth of Paul Fussell's observation on the war's impact on soldiers. The author of *The Great War in Modern Memory* asserted: "You learn that you have much wider dimensions than you had imagined before you had to fight a war. That's salutary. It's well to know exactly who you are, so you can conduct the rest of your life properly."[1]

Priests did indeed find wider dimensions in themselves and in their fellow soldiers through their experiences in the war. Priests who lived through the war had led, in the words of Teilhard de Chardin, "the quasi-collective life" with men they would never have previously met. They developed bonds of brotherhood by living with them and sharing the miseries of war. These bonds, they discovered, were based more on mutual respect than on shared faith. They also found in themselves a capacity for violence and for being swept up into the exaltation of battle, which strengthened their feelings of brotherhood and empathy for their fellows. As they developed what they called "virile friendships," they found themselves regarded as pastors and consolers by men who would otherwise never have looked to them for support. They had entered the war with feelings of patriotism despite the previous rejection they had experienced. They exited the war with a profound sense of identity with their countrymen and with their country.

It is clear from their memoirs and letters that the priests entered the war recognizing the suspicion in which they were held by their countrymen. They hoped their devotion to duty would prove their patriotism and their loyalty to France, and thus would earn them not only respect but also inclusion in the body politic. Abbé Jean Lagardère, who in his fifties became chaplain to a division in the Fourth Army, admitted that he went into battle dreaming of rehabilitating "the priest and religion by his example and thinking fondly of 'his sons.'"[2] On one occasion, he wrote that the head doctor, seeing him leaving for the trenches, said: "Ah! Chaplain, don't worry, come on now, they will not be more grateful to you for all that." This caused Lagardère to reflect on his motivation. He claimed that he was not going to the front out of audacity or imprudent heroism, but rather "to have the right, if he survives the war, to cry out to certain villains who will want to tyrannize us anew, that he is as French as they are and perhaps more than them. It is not for glory that he braves death: it is by temperament first, and then because he is the standard bearer for religion and because he wants to hold this standard high and firm, no matter the cost."[3]

A postwar article in the seminary bulletin, "Les Seminaristes de Saint-Sulpice Morts Pour La France," by Abbé Antoine Verriele, director of the seminary at Issy, confirms that many shared the hope that priests' sacrifices would earn reconciliation with France. He quoted Abbé Ligeard, who, he indicated, was "gloriously killed by the enemy." Before going to war, Ligeard had avowed that he offered his sacrifice in advance "in order to clear up the misunderstandings between the people of France and the priests." Verriele commented: "May the spectacle of this beautiful sacerdotal youth, giving itself with so much love in the clear freshness of its zeal, contribute to such a precious result! How beautiful are the first fruits of the holocaust of the priesthood of France! Where can one find such new impressions of ardent piety for God, of fervor for the Patrie? Nothing can better reveal to our heroic and generous nation the true soul of its priests."[4]

Similarly, the young seminarian Sgt. Pierre Babouard wrote that, despite his longing to be back in the seminary, he reminded himself daily that on the battlefront priests and seminarians were still "doing sacerdotal work, redemptive work for the salvation of France and the good of the Church." He hoped "that the sufferings borne in common with our soldiers will result in religious peace and that, from now on, all the bloody Masses offered by so many of our brothers, all the dreams so generously sacrificed of an apostolic future, will produce their fruits on earth as well as in heaven."[5]

They had been astonished by the ease with which they had developed friendships during the war. The Franciscan seminarian Thérésette described his friendship with a former member of the Chamber of Deputies, who had been under secretary of state. He wrote that they patrolled together in late 1914 in the area of Verdun and became "a solid pair of friends." He said that one day they shared a bottle of wine, which they had picked up during a daring reconnaissance. He commented: "Who would have chosen to say two years ago that a former Under Secretary of State would toast his glass so amicably with the glass of a dreadful Capuchin!"[6]

The thirty-seven-year-old stretcher-bearer Albert Bessières, in the hospital for a contusion on his foot, reflected as he was falling asleep one night: "I am happy to sleep among you as one of you. You work so hard, like you do at the front, to show me your respectful sympathy by addressing me in ways which affirm your desire to compensate for I know not what official bullying dimly perceived. You call me: 'Little father, grandfather, Monsieur l'abbé, Monsieur Chaplain.' I am only your older brother and have no more pride than that."[7]

Indeed it was this sense of brotherhood that gave meaning to the war for both the priests and soldiers in the postwar period.[8] Antoine Prost, who studied veterans' associations between World War I and the outbreak of World War II, asserted that the experience and memory of the brotherhood of the trenches was the most long-lasting feeling that gave meaning to the war experience for the veterans. He wrote: "Living means giving meaning to what one lives through. What is surprising, in this context, is the fact that veterans looked to fraternity and not to patriotism for validation of the deepest significance of their experience. Certainly it was for France that they fought in the early days of the war, but no abstract concept survived long in the face of the experience of war: it needed something more concrete, more immediate proof. . . . They held on because they knew that they owed it to themselves and were conscious of solidarity with their close companions."[9] To describe the roots of this feeling he cites a memoir in which a soldier explains that by 1916 disillusionment and weariness hung over everything and the meaning of life collapsed into a very narrow world. Instead, the soldier was fighting "out of integrity, habit, and strength . . . because he could not do otherwise. . . . His dwelling changed from a house into a dugout, his family into his fighting companions."[10]

Prost also maintains that the spotlight focused on brotherhood by the veterans was not only an attempt to portray their experience in a flattering way, but it "responded to the innermost and vital need to confer meaning on experience: particularly on one that was absurd and inhuman."[11] In experiencing a life-or-death ordeal, he maintains that one cannot tell oneself it was senseless. Instead, Prost attests that some soldiers made a deliberate decision to use religion to make sense of their life-or-death ordeal.

He quoted from the notebooks of a territorial officer, Tézenas du Montcel, "a lawyer from a respected family with 'correct attitudes.'" Montcel recounted arguing with a priest over the spiritual meaning of the war. He wrote on February 8, 1917: "Quite a long conversation with Father Plus [Raoul Plus, S.J., Jesuit chaplain of Montcel's 102d Territorial Infantry Regiment]. . . . He does not see the 'advantage' of the war from the religious angle: he does not find souls changed. . . . But I believe in virtue and the fruits of sacrifice. . . . I told him so, I believe it, but above all I want to believe it."[12]

Priests also shared with their fellow veterans the need to find religious meaning in the sufferings of war. Priests were perhaps even more inclined to use religious symbolism for both their roles in the war and for the endurance of their fellow soldiers. From the earliest days of the war, priests used religion to make sense of the awful carnage. They saw the war as a means of expiation for sin and as the path to redemption for themselves and their fellows, and for France. They compared the sufferings of the soldiers to those of Christ. True to this vision, the twenty-two-year old seminarian and sergeant Pierre Babouard wrote: "How many times, head smashed by an explosive, a poor comrade reminds me, by the bloody halo around his face, of the Divine Lord crowned with thorns! The death of Jesus saved the world. Will the death of our soldiers save France?" And in a reflection on the promise of resurrection, he continued: "And Christ Jesus, resuscitated and glorious, sent his apostles to conquer the world. Death is then the principal of life."[13]

In the same vein, on September 3, 1914, just before the battle in which he would be killed, the young seminarian from Angers, Jean Audouin, a sergeant for just a few days, wrote to his family: "Pray that, if it is for the glory of God, I will not fall in this mêlée. Pray for poor France. She has not lost, but she will expiate her sins in shedding very much blood. If the blood of victims who are a little purer is necessary, I will give mine in the greatest simplicity. It will be my first and last mass. But finally I will have played my role as victim and priest; I will have followed my Master. Let us go, let us abandon ourselves to the will of God."[14]

Charles Thellier de Poncheville, the forty-year-old chaplain, also compared the agony of the soldiers awaiting the battle to the agony of Christ in the

Garden of Gethsemane. He wrote: "Like Him, they have all felt their being troubled, revolted, protesting death. Their will strengthened heroically, as His, in memory of His." And like Him, he continued, they willingly went forward to face their executioners.[15]

These examples contradict Paul Fussell's firm assertion that by the time of the Great War, religion had lost its power to help men grapple with the horror of war.[16] Annette Becker quoted letters from regular soldiers offering their lives as sacrifice, as well as letters and books by Ernest Psichari and Henri Massis, who wrote of rediscovering the mystique of sacrifice.[17] Philip Jenkins argues that ultimately "the scale of violence was so incomprehensibly vast that only religious language was adequate to the chore of describing it, or justifying it."[18]

As the war progressed priests were asked their opinions on the possibility of reconciliation between church and state. Jules Leveque, a military chaplain at the Hopital Temporaire, Secteur 51, predicted an improvement in the position of the priest and the Church after the war. In a letter dated May 11, 1917, to Geoffroy de Grandmaison at the Bureau of Volunteer Chaplains, he predicted the future of relations between church and state would be changed by the interaction between priests and soldiers during the war. He wrote:

> I would not want to decide the famous question of knowing whether the war will have been more fatal than useful from the religious viewpoint, but I may be really able to affirm for all that I have seen personally that after the war the religious question will emerge in a different manner. One will be able to try to broach this grave matter in a more categorical manner without fear of seeming closed-minded or from another age. In the sick rooms where I spend each afternoon I greet soldiers who are always at least very polite but very often very cordial and they appear happy to be able to have a conversation for some time with someone who is concerned exclusively with their interests. The more experience in these intimate, familiar, and simple conversations with the soldiers, the more I am convinced that it is relatively easy enough to do good among them, at least to prepare the terrain on which others will be able later to sow the seeds of true supernatural fruit.[19]

Priests looked for signs that this reconciliation would come. Georges Sevin, stationed as a nurse at a hospital in Vincennes, wrote to his mother on September 13, 1915, that he was thrilled that the head doctor, a Protestant, had not only recommended him for a citation but in a short speech "pointed out the role of the priest, having to be the great consoler of the sick and the afflicted . . . , the priest who does not hesitate to change his cassock for the clothing of a soldier and runs to danger and death, if it is necessary to save his fellow soldier." He believed it was of the greatest significance that a Protestant superior would praise priests in front of all the soldiers. In a follow-up letter he claimed he was happy for the distinction for another reason: "How can one possibly contend, after so many beautiful citations concerning the clergy on the front, that it is we who have wanted the war . . . or that we are shirkers!"[20]

At least some of the priests realized that both they and Church authorities had a part to play in this hoped-for reconciliation. They felt that they had learned a good deal from their wartime exposure to men from all walks of life, and they expressed a desire to continue to reach out to them after the war. They spoke of a change in their methods of ministry that needed to take place.

Achille Liénart, who went on to a distinguished career as archbishop of Lille and later cardinal, fervently believed that he would "profit from the intimate knowledge of the popular soul acquired by the contact of all these days, to glorify God more and to worthily serve France in peace."[21] His biographer, Catherine Masson, believed that the war changed him in significant ways. She wrote that "the emotional dimension of the war experience, which characterizes the mentality of the veteran, was very marked in Achille Liénart." She believed that his experiences with the horrors of war made him dedicated to pursuing peace among men at every level. His direct contact with people from varying religious backgrounds, milieus, and races guided him in his pursuit of social action and of interreligious dialogue. He became known as "the cardinal of the workers," as well as a zealous advocate for ecumenism, before and throughout the Second Vatican Council.[22]

Jesuit stretcher-bearer Albert Bessières believed France would change, if priests continued after the war to work as arduously as they had during the Chemin des Dames offensive in 1917. He wrote: "Ah! If tomorrow, we the priests of France, if those at least, whom God allows to live . . . knew how to bring to that which was and remains . . . our unique vocation, the rescue of souls, the same energy, the same tension of all the human strength up to the point of exhaustion, the same inexorable will to succeed, the same decision, and the same imperious desire, the same speed of execution and the same contempt for fatigue, for risks . . . France would know, again, great days."[23]

At the end of the war, Teilhard de Chardin expressed his hopes for the future for the Church and mankind and the role he hoped to play. He wrote from Strasbourg on December 10, 1918:

> I'm delighted to agree that this year our common intention should be the one you suggest: to work and pray that our Lord, at the dawn of a new world-cycle, may descend among us ever more and more living. . . .
>
> There are some things that force me, when I come up against them, to summon up all the great incentives that urge one towards peaceful toler- ance, if I am not to give way to irritation. At the moment, the Church, or rather its administrators, have no understanding of what real life is. To do my own small part to create in her a movement towards progress would seem to me an excellent use of the period that's just beginning.[24]

In another letter dated December 15, 1918, he continued this line of thinking, stating that he was convinced that it was necessary for the Church to present dogma in a more real, universal way.[25] And on June 5, 1919, he told his cousin that he was collecting material to write an article entitled "Notes towards the Evangelization of New Times," in which he would provide a brief plan for an apostolate in the hope of initiating a "movement and bringing into being some schemes for practical institutions."[26]

Marie-Claude Flagéat, in her book on the Jesuits during the Great War, stated that the Jesuits fought for their country, for the return of the lost provinces to France, and for the reintegration of members of religious orders within French society. These hopes and more were certainly shared by the par- ish priests and the bishops of France.[27] During the war the Jesuits developed strategies to assure that priests held on to the affections they had earned among the men. Concerned about the real will of the veterans to fight for them after the war, they proposed various means to perpetuate the memory of the brotherhood of the trenches. As early as February 1917, Joseph Dassonville devised a project entitled Mémento de la Guerre, to provide soldiers with a portable memento when they or their chaplains were separated from the service. Albert Bessières proposed the formation of a Ligue des Vétérans to the readers of Frères d'Armes in the April 1, 1918, issue. He believed that in this league, former soldiers would continue to live the fraternity of the trenches. United for the defense of great interests, they would be able to impose a truly French program on legislative candidates.[28]

The Catholic press, for its part, believed that to win policies beneficial to the Church it was necessary to document the outstanding contributions of the clergy to the war. They assiduously portrayed the contributions of the clergy to the war effort throughout the war. They published letters from priests at the front describing their work. Their readers' responses inspired the editors with the idea of putting together a *Livre d'Or* to document the contributions of priests and religious to the war effort.

The project was solidified in response to what churchmen called the *rumeur infâme* (infamous rumor), the allegations that the priests had wanted the war and that the bishops had funded Germany. Rumors also alleged that even mobilized priests stayed out of harm's way on the battlefield. These rumors, which were spread by anticlerical newspapers and speeches throughout the small villages of France, convinced the editors of the Catholic press and the bishops that it was necessary to prove the patriotism of the clergy. In December 1914 the publishing house Bonne Presse asked Jean Guiraud to begin to write a book on the service of the clergy and the congregations, to be divided into two parts, one descriptive and one documentary. By March 31, 1915, *La Croix* announced the beginning of the work.[29]

The editors had already been collecting news of citations published in newspapers and comparing them with the *Journal Officiel* of the Ministry of War. From March onwards they established an active correspondence with mobilized priests and religious, with bishops, and with the families of those who had died on the battlefield, to obtain and verify information. They had hoped to publish the work in three volumes, but failed to obtain a minimum of three thousand subscriptions. Thus they decided to create two volumes of 1,260 pages each, to be sold for one hundred francs.[30]

They excluded the "simply mobilized" but included all the Catholic clergy and religious who died, were cited or decorated with military honors from all the Allied countries, France, Belgium, Italy, England, Canada, America, and Poland. They added the names of the bishops and Catholic priests of the oriental rites killed by the Turks during the war or decorated by the Allies. At the end of the second volume they placed, in alphabetical order, individual notices of those who had been forgotten or were honored after the publication of the volumes. Each entry includes the individual's ecclesiastical or religious designation, changes in military rank during the war, the different battles in which the person participated, and the text of citations and decorations.[31]

The statistics the editors accumulated were indeed impressive. Of the 23,418 parish priests who fought in the war, 3,101 were killed and 7,769 received 11,856 military citations and 9,793 decorations. The members of religious orders numbered 9,281 and of these 1,157 were killed, and 2,655 of them received 4,237 citations and 3,447 decorations.[32]

The bishops greeted the publication with enthusiasm, as exemplified in an address the bishop of Dijon, Mgr. Maurice Landrieux, gave at his Petit Séminaire on the occasion of distributing prizes. In emphasizing the importance of this recognition, he said:

> Our priests and our religious in the army, in the ranks like the others, have written, from 1914 to 1918, a beautiful chapter in the history of the war, but also a beautiful page in the history of the Church of France.
>
> Not only public opinion, military authority, but also the government has rendered them homage. It is a fact which is established and which has an incontestable apologetic value. There is a détente in the country, among the people, the working class and peasants; brutal, aggressive anticlericalism is no longer popular: this comes from that. Our adversaries have not disarmed. They seek, they wait for the opportunity, the means; the hate smolders, it would like to bite: it collides with this wall: the attitude of the priests and the religious during the war.
>
> And I say that no one has the right to remove a stone from this wall. I say that, on this earth, we are all united and that, from this viewpoint, your military medal should come out of the shadow and reclaim the full sunlight: . . . not for our personal satisfaction, but in the interest of this holy cause to which all here, up to the littlest ones, have consecrated our lives.[33]

Although public sentiment in the initial postwar period went far to fulfill the hopes of the priests and their superiors for a better rapport, government officials appeared unmoved, at least initially. They were determined to support a strict adherence to the policy of secularization. The first profound symbol of that policy was President Raymond Poincaré's refusal to attend a Te Deum at Notre Dame Cathedral on November 17, 1918, to celebrate the war's successful conclusion. Poincaré deferred to Prime Minister Georges Clemenceau's interpretation that, in the secular state created in 1905, public officials should not attend religious services, no matter the occasion. Although both Poincaré and the president of the Chamber of Deputies, Paul Deschanel, disagreed with Clemenceau, they only sent their wives. The archbishop of Paris, Cardinal Amette, was very disappointed. Presiding over the ceremony, he praised the men who died to bring victory and expressed regret at the absence "of those who are responsible for the destinies of our country and who are the voluntary or constrained victims of a legal convention of doubtful validity."[34]

The Republicans in the Chamber of Deputies also quickly affirmed that the laws they had passed to secularize the state and education were "sacrosanct." Some Catholics, including some bishops, wanted to fight this interpretation. Nonetheless, Cardinal Amette himself agreed to the language of compromise in the program of the right-wing National Bloc party, which took control of the Chamber of Deputies and formed a new government in November 1919. The compromise stated: "Secularization must be harmonized with the liberties and the rights of all citizens whatever their religious views and in this way religious peace will be assured to the country."[35]

The National Bloc, a coalition of right-wing parties that included many war veterans and devout Catholics, came to power with the elections of November 1919. Clemenceau had resisted restoring relations with the Vatican, although he had agreed that it would not be right to expel the religious who had returned to France to fight in the war. Clemenceau resigned as prime minister after losing his presidential bid in 1920. His successor, Alexandre Millerand, let it be known that he was in favor of reopening diplomatic relations with the Holy See. He also affirmed that members of religious orders who had returned to participate in the war should not be once more sent into exile. In a speech before the newly elected National Bloc he claimed: "I have declared for my part, it would appear impossible to me that, the war ended, one would escort to the border the religious who had crossed it to come to the front to take part in the dangers with their French brothers. . . . I simply ask that religious, like laymen, have the same right to assemble under the law, to uphold and to propagate their opinions. . . . The Republic of Victory is the property of all the French people. It has the right to be generous, liberal, and tolerant."[36]

The Vatican itself sincerely wanted diplomatic relationships restored, so Pope Benedict XV was open to compromise. Millerand sent a representative to the Vatican in March 1920 and by May there was an agreement. The Holy See went so far as to concede that it would not expect France to change laws relating to religious worship, teaching, and the right of association.

An agreement was also reached on the procedure the pope would follow in submitting episcopal appointments to the government. The measure to restore diplomatic relations with the Vatican was passed by parliament on November 30, 1920, by a vote of 391 to 179.

The Vatican further helped to create a favorable atmosphere for the resumption of relations by canonizing Joan of Arc a saint of the Catholic Church a few days after the initial agreement. It was only when the French bishops and cardinals attended the canonization services that they discovered that in the negotiations the pope had also reversed Pius X's position on religious associations. The more liberal Benedict XV finally could see the merits of allowing the church to hold property in this manner. Although the cardinals and bishops had themselves urged Pius X to agree to the formation of religious associations in 1905, the postwar prelates agreed only with "respectful resistance." These bishops, mostly appointed by Pius X, were suspicious of the Republic and believed that the pope was compromising the "imprescriptible rights of Catholicism." They felt that by reversing Pius X's decision, he would give French Catholics a bad impression. They were doubtful that the legal precedents set since 1906 would really guarantee that church associations would defer to episcopal authority in their operations. Benedict's decision meant that now the French dioceses would be able to begin to hold property, including houses for bishops and priests and other facilities to promote their work.[37]

The immediate postwar period witnessed progress in the hoped-for reconciliation between church and state in France, as well as in respect for the priests. Although the Chamber of Deputies had affirmed that the secular laws were still sacrosanct, some were no longer applied and others were enforced with moderation. The religious orders, dissolved under the law of 1901, returned. Their members, who had been forced to abandon teaching under the law of 1904, returned to teach in the schools and colleges they had earlier relinquished to the care of secular priests (priests who were not members of religious orders) or lay staffs.[38]

More public demonstrations of this new relationship occurred in communities across the country. Local officials invited veteran priests to participate in local memorial services for their fallen brethren. The presence of these priests at public memorials, according to Annette Becker, seemed as natural to participants as it had been on the battlefield. Both during and after the war, unprecedented crowds gathered at cemeteries on November 1, the religious feast of All Saints, which was traditionally a day to honor the dead. The coincidence of the November armistice reinforced the religious link and emphasized the importance of that feast. The Republic's strict policy of separation of church and state also was disregarded in the government's use of the cross, the symbol of Christianity, to mark the graves of deceased soldiers. It too seemed natural for, it was, after all, "the sign of death in western Europe" and "always expressed" respect for the dead.[39]

Priests reinforced their special role in honoring the dead by providing rubrics for public memorial services, including speeches and texts. Mgr. Charles Ginisty—the author of a book on Verdun, *Paroles de Guerre*, published in 1919—was one of many. He detailed all the ingredients of rituals to be held at battlefield chapels and war memorials. He provided prayers for funeral services and family reunions. He actually wrote this book several weeks before the battle for Verdun, predicting both victory and revenge for the defeat of 1870.[40]

Although Catholics had been disappointed in the secular nature of the celebration of victory on July 14, 1919, and the ceremony of burying the unknown soldier under the Arc de Triomphe on November 11, 1920, Catholic bishops were appeased by 1920 because of the restoration of relations with the Vatican. Even though the archbishop of Paris was only allowed to bless the coffin of the unknown soldier, which was to be buried in the afternoon of October 29, 1920, Cardinal Luçon of Reims sent a letter to all French bishops, advising them to participate in the various local festivities by means of religious ceremonies. In this way, he asserted, they would demonstrate their appreciation of the benevolent attitude of the present government. He was referring specifically to the rapprochement between France and the Vatican, which had been confirmed with the Doulcet-Gasparri agreement on the exchange of a papal nuncio and an ambassador on May 28, 1920. Becker believes that by participating fully in the ceremonies of November 11, 1920, the authorities of the Catholic Church pressed their advantage and won final approval in the Chamber of Deputies of the reestablishment of the French embassy in the Vatican on November 30.[41]

In addition to their role in memorializing the dead, the sense of brotherhood and respect for the veteran was the basis for the growing inclusion of priests into the public life of France. It was in this spirit of brotherhood that municipal and prefectorial officials, as well as former commanders and many veterans, began to attend the public ceremonies for the installation of bishops who had fought in the war. Prewar sectarian tension was replaced by memories of mutual support in the face of shared danger. For the priests it was another sign of their renewed position in French society. In his study of the French episcopate in the postwar period, Frédéric Le Moigne recounts the first time municipal and prefectorial officials attended an episcopal installation. Mgr. Maurice Feltin, who had been an officer during the war, held his ceremony as bishop of Troyes at a war memorial. In his discourse Feltin remarked: "At the front, we were profoundly united whatever were our opinions. In addressing you for the first time, I ask you to continue this beautiful union."[42]

Le Moigne provides statistics that demonstrate that the vast majority of bishops selected in the postwar period, 79 out of 115, were veterans of the war. Further, he states that most of them had not been official chaplains, but rather were stretcher-bearers or ambulance workers, or were in the infantry and sometimes in the artillery. They were between the ages of twenty-five and forty during the war. A majority were in the military classes between 1889 and 1905 and therefore automatically served in the health service of the army. This would have placed them in the daily life of the soldiers, much more than the chaplains would have been.[43]

In witness to their affection, common soldiers applauded when their former priest comrades were promoted to the episcopate. A group of fellow soldiers sent a pectoral cross as a gift to Mgr. Lamy of Amiens with the inscription, "À notre camarade, Frédéric Lamy."[44] The bulletin of the veterans of the 39th Infantry Regiment commented on the nomination of Georges Choquet to the bishopric of Langres, stating that "everyone remembered the very great largesse of spirit that made him so friendly with all the poilus no matter what their religious opinions."[45]

Le Moigne suggests these bishops spoke eloquently to a generational memory. Everywhere in France the newly installed bishops, who were former combatants, understood the bonds and the solidarity established in the trenches and meant to profit by it to expand the spirit of entente.[46] Both bishops and priests reinforced their positions as what Le Moigne calls "agents of the cult of memory" through their roles as chaplains of regimental veterans' associations, which were vital in continuing a sense of community and memory. Like the future bishop of Périgueux who led the veterans of the

329th Infantry Regiment to battlefield sites where they had lost comrades, many priests organized such pilgrimages.[47]

Catherine Masson affirmed Achille Liénart's lifelong special relationship with the members of the 201st Infantry. In her introduction to his war journal, she states that he continued to meet with them throughout his life. She wrote: "He was always happy to greet them when he met them again in detours he made during his pastoral visits or when he took part in their family life (marriages, births, baptisms sometimes, funerals, etc.)." The bonds woven on the battlefield were present even as late as 1973 when veterans participated in Liénart's funeral ceremonies.[48]

These bonds of brotherhood, loyalty, and mutual respect that the priests had built up during the war proved to hold fast during the crisis caused by the renewed anticlerical policies proposed by the Cartel des Gauches. This coalition, which won control of the Chamber of Deputies after the elections of 1924, was similar to the one that had passed the anticlerical legislation in the early twentieth century. It was composed of both Radical Republicans and Socialists. Édouard Herriot became prime minister and outlined the first aims of his government on July 17, 1924. He stated that he wanted to give the country a "social peace" by amnesty for those who had been deserters during the war, but at the same time he rekindled the old sectarian wars. He announced that he intended to close the new French embassy at the Vatican and to apply the law relating to religious orders. Despite earlier government promises, he announced that the full body of secular legislation would be applied to the newly re-acquired territories of Alsace and Lorraine, where Germans had honored the 1801 Concordat after the 1870 conquest.[49]

Catholics mobilized quickly throughout France, but especially in Alsace and Lorraine. Numerous protest meetings in Obernai, Colmar, Mulhouse, Metz, and Strasbourg, and resolutions passed by municipal and departmental councils, caused Herriot to back down precipitately on his plans for Alsace and Lorraine.[50] The Jesuit former chaplain Paul Doncoeur and his colleagues also responded very quickly with an editorial in *Études* on July 20, entitled "Le tocsin qui sonne" ("The tocsin which sounds"). He stated: "Thus amnesty is prepared for the number of rebels, and without doubt some traitors, but condemnations are readied for the Frenchmen and Frenchwomen, who, as faithful to their country as to their God, returned to serve at that perilous moment."[51]

Jesuit Albert Bessières, former stretcher-bearer, called for a "Union catholique" for the defense of the threatened liberties in *Études* of October 20. Shortly thereafter he met with General Édouard de Castelnau, chief of the General Staff under General Joseph Joffre, who had two sons killed in the war. The general agreed to head up the movement called the Fédération Nationale Catholique (FNC, National Catholic Federation), founded in January 1925. Supporters quickly organized at the local and regional level with the formal approval of Church leaders. In late 1924 veterans from religious orders formed two organizations, the Ligue des Droits des Religieux Anciens Combattants (DRAC; League for the Rights of Religious Veterans) and the Ligue des Prêtres Anciens Combattants (PAC; League of Veteran Priests).[52]

By the end of 1924 the groups stimulated demonstrations across France. Bishops, senators, deputies, and other officials came together by the thousands, calling for religious peace. The first demonstration, on October 5, took place in La Roche-sur-Yon, followed by Toulouse on October 25, Rodez on the October 26, and continued in most of the larger as well as the smaller cities throughout November and December. These included Bordeaux, Avignon, Lyon, Tours, and Reims. The largest of these demonstrations took place in Folgoët in the Finistère on December 8, 1924, where 52,000 persons gathered near the basilica to protest against the policies of the Herriot government. The bishop of Quimper and Léon, General de Castelnau, a senator, and three deputies all took turns speaking. Mayors and priests from nearby towns took part along with the crowd, brandishing placards against the expulsion of religious and the closing of free schools in Alsace-Lorraine.[53]

As their memberships and demonstrations increased, worried public officials monitored their activities. The FNC had 82 diocesan groups by early 1925. Membership in the various organizations reached 1,832,000 by September 1926. From October 1924 to the end of the year, the groups held 392 public meetings, published monthly bulletins, and inaugurated a campaign of lectures.[54] DRAC blanketed the country with posters and tracts with such titles as "L'indignation d'un ancien combattant" ("The indignation of veterans") and "Nous ne partirons pas" ("We will not leave") by Paul Doncoeur, and "Des congrégations en France . . . Pourquoi pas?" ("Religious orders in France . . . Why not?") by Abbé Thellier de Poncheville.[55]

Paul Doncoeur was most active in the movement and became one of its most famous figures. With his battle cry, "Nous ne partirons pas," he crisscrossed France giving speeches to enthusiastic audiences. There is a note from the minister of the interior to the minister of war, labeled "confidential" and dated "Paris, February 20, 1925," which complains that Doncoeur, as principal speaker at a political meeting in Avignon on February 10, was particularly violent in his attack on the religious policy of the government. What most troubled the minister, however, was the attendance of soldiers and noncommissioned officers in military uniform and of the commander of the 7th Regiment of Engineers, Colonel Mevel, in civilian clothes.

A report on a meeting in the Grande Salle at the recreational Luna Park, on the outskirts of Paris near the Porte Maillot on December 16, 1925, organized by DRAC and PAC, asserted that eight thousand persons attended. An article from the Catholic newspaper, *L'Écho de Paris* claimed there were 20,000. General de Castelnau attended and the speaker was former official chaplain Abbé Daniel Bergey, who had been elected to the Chamber of Deputies from the Department of Gironde. A great number of elected officials and well-known personalities attended. Bergey, famous for his oratorical skills, asked the crowd to fight the laic laws, and proclaimed the union between the regular (members of religious orders) and the secular clergy. He congratulated the Alsatians, many of whose deputies and senators were seated on the stage, for rallying the spiritual forces of France. He affirmed that they wanted peace, but would conduct war if Caesar wanted it. When Doncoeur took the podium, the audience greeted him with cries of "Vive Doncoeur!" and his own slogan, "Nous ne partirons pas." At the end of his presentation there was loud and prolonged applause.[56]

The meeting at Luna Park and other meetings were held even after Herriot's government fell on April 10, 1925, and was replaced by Paul Painlevé, who did not pursue the same policies. His minister of foreign affairs, Aristide Briand, maintained the French embassy at the Vatican. The DRAC held its first general assembly on June 14, 1925. According to an article in the June 15, 1925, issue of *Liberté*, thirty-five regional groups participated. Cardinal Dubois of Paris celebrated mass at Montmartre in memory of religious, priest, and Catholic combatants dead on the field of honor. Hundreds of priests were joined by former combatants and friends in a procession to the Arc de Triomphe, where a religious, blind from the war, lit the flame of honor. The official report described the meeting as peaceful and energetic and noted that the closing procession to the Arc de Triomphe passed through the middle of a sympathetic crowd. There were shouts of "Bravo!" and of "There they are, the ones Herriot wanted to banish." The author of the report wrote that speakers during the day claimed that the new tone of the Painlevé ministry meant victory: "The threatened religious congratulated themselves in front of a sympathetic crowd for having protected the cause of the 'religious' under the most surely accepted aegis of 'former religious combatant.'"[57]

An official governmental report detailed the DRAC's plans for the following year, 1926. First there would be a mass for the religious who died on the field of honor, celebrated at the Basilica of Montmartre, with a speech by Abbé Bergey. After meetings and a banquet, the members would assemble at the Georges V metro station on the Champs Elysées and form a column with priests and religious mutilated or decorated in the war in the lead, followed by delegates from Paris and from the suburbs, to march to the Arc de Triomphe. There they would relight the flame at the tomb of the unknown soldier. They had plans to assure order and predicted many members of the public would attend, making an escort for the veteran priests as they processed to the Arc de Triomphe. After the event, *La Croix*, on June 24, 1926, described "a triumphal day." Crowds greeted the religious veterans, yelling, "Vivent les religieux!" and, "Ils ne partiront pas!"[58]

Thus it seemed that in 1926, the priests had succeeded in renegotiating their position within French society. Although the laic laws were never abrogated they were not enforced. In the 1950s when Léonce Raffin, who had served as stretcher-bearer then as a volunteer chaplain in the war, gathered his war notebooks for publication, he assessed the lasting effects of "union sacrée:"

The most opposite spirits have fraternized faced with the national peril. Religious prejudices have fallen; the suspicions of the ostracism the priests suffered for forty years vanished. We recognize that today some of them remain. We, the old ones, experience no more the sharp and insulting laicism. Alas! That does not include adherence to the religion of Christ for the sons and grandsons of the combatants. The most solid, the most generous, the most ardent in faith among the combatants have been decimated by this bloody war; and the weakening of morals, which followed it, has brought ravages to families and delayed the uniting of souls in the traditional religion of the country. But let us not despair. It cannot be in vain that the blood of the best has been spilt.

It keeps its redemptive quality. Our Christian heroes have died with conviction. A priest, killed on the battlefield of Ypres in December, 1914 wrote: ". . . To shed one's blood for the Church, for France, for friends, for all those who carry in their hearts the same ideals as I do, and for all the others also so that they may know the joy of believing. Ah! how beautiful it is. . . . " God cannot be deaf to such wishes of these, priests and laymen, who have signed them with their blood.[59]

This odyssey of the priests during the war undoubtedly caused a profound change in the relationship between the priests and their fellow citizens. Although they might still wish for a widespread return to the Catholic faith, the priests had come to a realization that they had respect and value in the eyes of their countrymen, despite the measure of religious practice. In turn, their brothers in arms and their families might not raise practicing Catholics but they would not allow the priests to become the pariahs they had been by the end of the nineteenth century.

The words of Paul Doncoeur reverberate for the entire clergy: "Since then, the religious are full-fledged Frenchmen."[60]

CONCLUSION

This study of the odyssey of French priests at war recounts a tale of both personal and societal transformation. It adds a new dimension to our understanding of how World War I changed history. As a study of the personal testimonies of French priests mobilized to serve in World War I, it adds new and unique voices to that war's narrative. It allows an exploration of the question of how men schooled for the altar adapted to the battlefield, and in so doing explores several significant issues. These include: the power of societal values of patriotism and of bravery entwined with concepts of masculinity; the seduction of the battlefield and the spirit of revenge; the role and place of religion in World War I among the priests and soldiers of France.

The determined secularization of the Third Republic required priests to serve in the military. Although it would have been difficult to defy government authority, the historical context helped motivate both the bishops and priests to quickly comply in 1914. They were anxious to prove their loyalty to France, which had been seriously impugned by anticlerical rhetoric during the last half of the nineteenth century. They were not immune to the heightened patriotism generated by a German threat so reminiscent of the humiliating defeat in 1870. There was also widespread concern about the decline of virile ideals of bravery and physical vigor in both Europe and the United States in the years before the war. Many believed that war would redeem callow youth who had been caught up in effeminate pleasures. For churchmen, the concern for the disappearance of men from church services fanned similar fears that religion itself was becoming feminized.

The priests' wartime experiences illustrate the truth of Paul Fussell's observation that individuals who fight a war find out things about themselves they would never have learned. As they joined the troops in the barracks, the priests were pleasantly surprised that it was easy and comfortable to adapt their habits of clerical discipline to those of the military. But they were shocked to find themselves caught up in the enthusiasm of battle and excited by killing the enemy. Combatants and noncombatants alike spoke of feeling "more alive" at the front and conversely depressed when in the rear. They welcomed the feeling of comradeship that developed among their fellow soldiers and embraced the new "virile friendships" they made, which were in stark contrast to their lives in parish churches. Their reactions illustrate the observation that war provokes the most basic instincts of every human. Men on the battlefield, even men schooled for the altar, become totally caught up in a world in which survival for themselves and their fellows becomes the ultimate concern.

Even as the priests identified with their fellow soldiers, they were able to merge their religious values with the goals of the war. They found meaning in sacrifice, creatively comparing sacrifice for one's country to Christ's sacrifice of himself for the redemption of mankind. The priests saw their own and their comrades' sufferings on the battlefield as redemptive, just as Christ's had been, redemptive both for the individual and for the French nation. As much as they could, they tried to share this understanding with the men, to bolster their courage and determination to keep fighting. Many commanders found their services invaluable in supporting the morale of the troops, underlining the link between religion and war in this conflict.

The study of the priests' personal accounts of the war is important to our understanding of just how the long-acknowledged improvement of the relationship between the Catholic Church and the postwar government developed. It is evident from their correspondence that priests hoped that their services in the war would pave the way for this development. Their letters and observations demonstrate that it was not only their service but also a change in their attitudes toward their fellow soldiers that engendered a new mutual acceptance. Although the aspirations of the priests to be missionaries on the battlefield never waned, they became more realistic. They understood that they were earning respect by their service from men who might never become devout Christians. They adapted their traditional pastoral roles to wartime circumstances, serving the soldiers as confidants and consolers, while identifying with them as brothers in arms. They were assiduous in caring for the wounded, burying the dead, marking graves, and holding memorial services for fallen comrades. All of these activities endeared them to the men, regardless of their religious beliefs.

By their service to their country and to their fellow soldiers, they also earned respect from families on the home front who sought news of their loved ones, and a proper, marked gravesite for their dead. These very personal interactions became, to a large degree, the grounds for a new relationship between the French government and the Roman Catholic Church. From the earliest postwar period, even politicians as famously anticlerical as Clemenceau admitted that it would be impossible to exile again the members of religious orders who had served with such distinction on the battlefield.

This change was reflected in a number of ways. On the international level, the French government restored diplomatic relations with the Vatican and set up an embassy in Rome within two years of the war's ending. More remarkably, although Republicans declared the anticlerical laws "sacrosanct" immediately after the war, it was impossible to enforce them. Newly confident priest veterans were able to organize their fellow veterans and large segments of the population to resist Prime Minister Herriot's threat to expel religious orders and close religious schools. The demonstrations of 1926 garnered millions of participants; this contrasted sharply with the sparse demonstrations and strong electoral support for anticlerical politicians in the 1880s and in 1905. On the local level, mayors and prefects invited priests to play prominent roles in activities commemorating and honoring soldiers who had died in battle. Instead of being shunned and devalued as they had been for years, they now were treated as important members of the community.

The story of the Church and the veteran priests after 1926 is beyond the scope of my current research. However, there is much evidence that both the priests and the bishops understood that a new relationship had been formed and they worked to sustain it. Priests and bishops led pilgrimages to battle sites and gravesites. They were actively involved both in veterans' organizations and in the family lives of old comrades. Their new understanding also influenced their approach to ministry. They created missionary parishes and revived specialized Catholic Action and the worker-priest movement, all reforms that harkened back to suggestions of the priests' Congresses held before the war.

Ultimately, the story of French priests in World War I is important on a number of levels. It adds new voices to the conversation concerning the memory of World War I and the ways in which participants came to grapple with its meaning and were changed by the experience. At the same time it documents, through personal testimony, the transformations that helped mitigate the antagonism between the Roman Catholic Church and the Third Republic and promote feelings of mutual respect between priests and the French people, and recognition of national identity.

NOTES

Introduction

1. Jean-Jacques Becker, ed., *Histoire culturelle de la Grande Guerre* (Paris: A. Colin, 2005), 7–8.

2. André Font-Réaulx, *René de la Perraudière, novice de la Compagnie de Jésus, sergent d'infanterie française, mort au champ d'honneur* (Toulouse: l'Apostolat de la Prière, 1918), 36.

3. Letter from Jesuit Captain Frédéric de Bélinay, October 19, 2016 cited in Pierre Teilhard de Chardin, *The Making of a Mind: Letters from a Soldier Priest, 1914–1919*, trans. René Hague (New York: Harper and Row, 1965), 136.

4. Teilhard de Chardin, *The Making of a Mind*, 183.

5. Achille Liénart and Catherine Masson, *La guerre de 1914–1918 vue par un aumônier militaire* (Villeneuve d'Ascq: Presses Universitaires du Septentrion, 2008), 118.

6. Jacques Fontana, *Les catholiques français pendant la Grande Guerre* (Paris: Editions du Cerf, 1990); Xavier Boniface, *L'aumônerie militaire français, 1914–1962* (Paris: Cerf, 2001); Xavier Boniface, "L'aumônerie militaire francaise, 1914–1962," PhD thesis, University of Lille, 1992; Nadine-Josette Chaline, "Les aumôniers catholiques dans l'armée française" in *Chrétiens dans la première guerre mondiale* (Paris: Cerf, 1993); Annette Becker, *War and Faith: The Religious Imagination in France, 1914–1930*, trans. Helen McPhail (Oxford: Berg, 1998); Joan L. Coffey, "For God and France: The Military Law of 1889 and the Soldiers of Saint-Sulpice," *Catholic Historical Review* 88, no. 4 (2002): 679–85; Geoffroy de Grandmaison and François Veuillot, *L'aumônerie militaire pendant la guerre, 1914–1918* (Paris: Bloud et Gay, 1923); Marie-Claude Flagéat, *Les jésuites français dans la Grande Guerre, témoins, victimes, héros, apôtres* (Paris: Cerf, 2008); Daniel Moulinet, *Prêtres soldats dans la Grande Guerre: Les clercs bourbonnais sous les drapeaux* (Rennes: Presse Universitaire de Rennes, 2014); Joseph F. Byrnes, "The Limits of Personal Reconciliation: Priests and *Instituteurs* in World War I," in *Catholic and French Forever: Religious and National Identity in Modern France*

(University Park: Pennsylvania State University Press, 2005). Alain Toulza, *La Grande Guerre des hommes de Dieu: Héros des tranchées, entre persécutions et Union sacrée* (Paris: DRAC, 2015). Léonce de Grandmaison, in *Impressions de guerre de prêtres soldats* (Paris: Plon-Nourrit, 1917), provides excerpts from letters from priests in the war, mostly without providing the names of the correspondents because of concerns about security during the war. André Ducasse, in *La guerre racontées par les combattants* (Paris: E. Flammarion, 1932), provides brief excerpts from accounts he deems "authentic" rather than "official," written by soldiers, officers, and some priests. Stéphane Audoin-Rouzeau, in *Men at War, 1914–1918: National Sentiment and Trench Journalism in France during the First World War* (Oxford: Berg, 1992), analyzes newspapers published by soldiers, exploring the motivations at the roots of their commitment to the war, despite its unceasing horror.

7. Leonard V. Smith, in *Embattled Self: French Soldier Testimony of the Great War* (Ithaca, N.Y.: Cornell University Press, 2008), focuses on soldiers' narratives that attempt to find meaning in the war beyond the "meta-narrative" of trauma and tragedy that has emerged. Martha Hanna's *Your Death Would Be Mine: Paul and Marie Pireaud in the Great War* (Cambridge, Mass.: Harvard University Press, 2006) also demonstrates that artilleryman Pireaud believed in the French cause despite being horrified by the extermination of the battlefield.

8. Jonathan H. Ebel, *Faith in the Fight: Religion and the American Soldier in the Great War* (Princeton, N.J.: Princeton University Press, 2010), 3.

9. Ebel, *Faith in the Fight*, 7–9; Raymond Jonas, *The Tragic Tale of Claire Ferchaud and the Great War* (Berkeley: University of California Press, 2005), 4; George L. Mosse, *Fallen Soldiers: Reshaping the Memory of the World Wars* (New York: Oxford University Press, 1990).

10. Étienne Fouilloux, "Première Guerre Mondiale et Changement Religieux en France" in Jean Jacques Becker, *Histoire culturelle de la Grande Guerre* (Paris: A. Colin, 2005), 117–18, 122–23. His references are: Dominique Avon and Gérard Cholvy, *Paul Doncœur, S.J. (1880–1961): Un croisé dans le siècle* (Paris: Les Éditions du Cerf, 2001); Corinne Bonafoux-Verrax, "La Fédération nationale catholique, 1924–1944" (thèse inédite de l'Institut d'études politiques de Paris, 1999); Jacqueline Lalouette, *La libre pensée en France, 1848–1940* (Paris: Albin Michel, 1997); Annette Becker, *La guerre et la foi: De la mort à la mémoire, 1914–1930* (Paris: Armand Colin, 1994).

11. Frédéric Le Moigne, "Groupes et individus dans l'épiscopat français au milieu du vingtième siècle (1930–1935)" (PhD diss., Université de Rennes 2, 2000), 53.

12. Byrnes, *Catholic and French Forever*, 147–54.

13. *La preuve du sang: Livre d'or du clergé et des congrégations, 1914–1922*, 2 vols. (Paris: Bonne Presse, 1925–1930) [This reference refers to two print volumes I used during my research. The entire work has been made available in a downloadable PDF format for the centennial of World War I by the Diocèse aux armées françaises, https://dioce-seauxarmees.fr/la-preuve-du-sang-le-livre-d-or.html, last consulted on May 11, 2017.]; Jean Norton Cru, *Témoins: Essai d'analyse et de critique des souvenirs de combattants édités en français de 1915 à 1928* (Paris: Les Etincelles, 1929). I used Cru's work for

purposes of verifying the publications rather than for his criticism of the attitudes of the writers. The quarrels over Cru's critiques, particularly of memoirs that glorify war, are thoroughly described by Leonard Smith in "Jean Norton Cru et la subjectivité de l'objectivité," in Becker, *Histoire culturelle de la Grande Guerre*, 89–100.

14. *La preuve du sang*, 1:xlv.

15. John McManners, *Church and State in France, 1870–1914* (New York: Harper & Row, 1972), 168.

16. Joan Wallach Scott, *The Politics of the Veil* (Princeton, N.J.: Princeton University Press, 2007), 15.

Chapter 1. The Anticlerical Third Republic

1. My purpose in this chapter is to provide examples of the alienation, which developed between the French Catholic priest and the general public during the Third Republic. I am not attempting to reinterpret the quarrels between the Catholic Church and the Third Republic but simply to describe how these political and social developments shaped the position of Catholic priests in French society. Several historians have focused on the conflicts between church and state in the nineteenth century using the currently popular term "culture wars." Frederick Brown, in *For the Soul of France: Culture Wars in the Age of Dreyfus* (New York: Alfred A. Knopf, 2010), dramatizes the conflicts between the Catholic Church and the French state by focusing on the events that provoked the most vitriolic and uncompromising political discourse. In his approach, he fails to look at the periodic efforts at reconciliation and attempts on both sides to adapt to contemporary circumstances. A different, more balanced approach can be found in the edited work of Christopher Clark and Wolfram Kaiser, *Culture Wars: Secular-Catholic Conflict in Nineteenth-Century Europe* (Cambridge, UK: Cambridge University Press, 2003). They contend that the conflict over the place of religion in the polity was played out in different scenarios all across Western Europe and that it ultimately represents an intermittently bitter but ultimately productive argument between and among the various groups as they attempted to adjust to the challenges of political, social, and economic change.

2. Arthur Mugnier, Marcel Billot and Jean d'Hendecourt, *Journal de l'abbé Mugnier: 1879–1939* (Paris: Mercure de France, 1985), entry March 7, 1880, 27.

3. An example of the impact of this restriction was that the size of the average parish in Paris increased four-fold between 1802 and 1900, from 5,431 to 23,360. Maurice Larkin, *Church and State after the Dreyfus Affair: The Separation Issue in France* (New York: Harper & Rowe, 1974), 58–59.

4. Evelyn Acomb observed that, given the history of the Catholic Church's fate when a monarchical government was not in power, it was "only natural" for the greater number of bishops and priests to be monarchists. Evelyn M. Acomb, *The French Laic Laws (1879–1889): The First Anti-Clerical Campaign of the Third French Republic* (New York: Columbia University Press, 1941), 22–23. Thomas Kselman, *Miracles and Prophecies in Nineteenth-Century France* (New Brunswick, N.J.: Rutgers University Press, 1983), 33.

5. Réné Rémond, *The Right Wing in France: From 1815 to de Gaulle*, 2nd and rev. ed., trans. James M. Laux (Philadelphia: University of Pennsylvania Press, 1969), 172.

6. McManners, *Church and State*, 40.

7. Ibid., 43–44.

8. Christopher Clark maintains that the "Romanization" of the Catholic Church was a Europe-wide phenomenon that was not only fostered by Rome's policies but also aided by state policies. He wrote: "A state that pressed the church hard naturally strengthened the hand of the ultramontanes, since it alienated observant Catholics from those (anti-ultramontane) elements within the senior clergy who favored a far-reaching accommodation to the demands of secular governments." Clark and Kaiser, "The New Catholicism and the European Culture Wars," in *Culture Wars*, 21.

9. Jacqueline Lalouette, *La république anticléricale XIXe–XXe siècles* (Paris: Éditions du Seuil, 2002), 9n1. Her source is *La république française*, 28 janvier 1876. Rémond, in *L'Anticlericalisme* (178), cites Léon Gambetta and Joseph Reinach, *Discours et plaidoyers politiques de M. Gambetta: Publiés par M. Joseph Reinach*, vol. 3 (Paris: G. Charpentier, 1880), 191. Rémond also cites several other of Gambetta's speeches with similar sentiments in *L'anticlericalisme* (178–83); McManners, *Church and State*, 41.

10. McManners, *Church and State*, 19.

11. Kselman, in *Miracles and Prophecies* (25–36), provides a detailed account of this phenomenon. He states that although, data on the involvement of clergy with local shrines is incomplete, some studies show that there was a major revival of interest in pilgrimages encouraged by the Church, starting with the cholera epidemic of 1849 and continuing through the 1860s. Figures gathered on Marian pilgrimages indicate a peak during the Second Empire of 134, and a decline to 72 during the first two decades of the Third Republic. But Kselman states that there was "a general movement within the Church to promote folkloric behavior provided it was supervised by responsible clergy." This resulted in increased requests for miraculous healing (36). Eugen Weber, in *Peasants into Frenchmen: The Modernization of Rural France, 1870–1914* (Stanford, Calif.: Stanford University Press, 1976, 346, 352–53), asserts that for whatever reason, the rural world was eager for miracles and when there were none they invented them. Clark and Kaiser, in *Culture Wars* (11) assert that the increase in popular religious devotions accompanied by the rise in religious associations, newspapers, and journals testify to the development of a "New Catholicism" across Europe and was an adaptation to the modern era that helped to motivate some of the friction between church and state.

12. Anita Rasi May, "The Falloux Law, the Catholic Press and the Bishops: Crisis of Authority in the French Church," *French Historical Studies* 8, no.1 (1973): 77–94.

13. Joseph Brugerette, *Le prêtre français et la societe contemporaine*, vol. 2, *Vers la séparation de l'église et de l'état (1871–1908)* (Paris: P. Léthielleux, 1938), vi; Weber, in *Peasants into Frenchmen* (357–59), states that the declining role of the priest was "fairly wide and welcome" and he gives examples of the resentment over fees for all the essential rites of passage, baptism, marriage, and funerals. Places in Church cost money and even the rights to carry statues and banners in processions were auctioned off.

14. Theodore Zeldin, "The Conflict of Moralities: Confession, Sin, and Pleasure in the Nineteenth Century," in *Conflicts in French Society: Anticlericalism, Education, and Morals in the Nineteenth Century*, ed. Theodore Zeldin (London: George Allen and Unwin, 1970), 13, 49.

15. Roger Magraw, "The Conflict in the Villages: Popular Anticlericalism in the Isère (1852–1870)," in Zeldin, *Conflicts in French Society*, 175–76.

16. Jean-Marie Mayeur, *Un prêtre démocrate: L'abbé Lemire, 1853–1928* (Paris-Tournai: Casterman, 1968), 31. Mayeur cites his source as the notebooks of Lemire, which he lists as follows: Cahiers, I, 1876, 303.

17. Mayeur, *Un prêtre démocrate*, 30. Cahiers, I, 1876, 332; Rémond, in *L'anticlericalisme* (27–28) states that it was a common belief among anticlericals that priests lived on the honest work of others.

18. Mugnier, Billot, and d'Hendecourt, *Journal*, entry September 6, 1880, 32–33.

19. McManners, *Church and State*, 9–10; Weber, *Peasants into Frenchmen*, 361.

20. Larkin, *The Separation Issue*, 7–9. Children would have already made their first communion between the ages of seven and ten, but this was a private family affair.

21. McManners, *Church and State*, 27–29; Mayeur, *Un prêtre démocrate*, 21–22.

22. McManners, *Church and State*, 45; Rémond, *L'anticlericalisme*, 121.

23. McManners, *Church and State*, 52.

24. Larkin, *The Separation Issue*, 26.

25. McManners, *Church and State*, 48–49; Rémond, *L'anticlericalisme*, 31.

26. Mugnier, Billot, and d'Hendecourt, *Journal*, entry June 29, 1880, 29.

27. McManners, *Church and State*, 51.

28. Ibid., xx and 59.

29. Archives Historiques de l'Archevêché de Paris, Serie 5 B II 7. Service Militaire du Clergé et dispenses; Adrien Dansette, *Religious History of Modern France*, vol. 2, *Under the Third Republic*, trans. John Dingle (New York: Herder and Herder, 1961), 56. For a lengthier description of the law requiring military service for seminarians and its impact, see Joan L. Coffey, "For God and France," 679–85.

30. Coffey, "For God and France," 680–81.

31. McManners, *Church and State*, 53.

32. Dansette, *Under the Third Republic*, 86–87.

33. McManners, *Church and State*, 65.

34. Larkin, *The Separation Issue*, 63 and Rémond, *L'anticlericalisme*, 201–6.

35. Larkin, *The Separation Issue*, 70–72; Benjamin F. Martin, *Count Albert de Mun, Paladin of the Third Republic* (Chapel Hill: University of North Carolina Press, 1978), 116–18, 135.

36. Larkin, *The Separation Issue*, 80–82.

37. Ibid., 85–86.

38. Ibid., 82–83.

39. McManners, *Church and State*, 130.

40. Larkin, *The Separation Issue*, 92.

41. Ibid., 98–99; Dansette, *Under the Third Republic*, 201–3.

42. Larkin, *The Separation Issue*, 99–100; Dansette, *Under the Third Republic*, 203–5.

43. McManners, *Church and State*, 142–43.

44. Ibid., 147–48; Dansette, *Under the Third Republic*, 229–30.

45. McManners, *Church and State*, 161–62.

46. Ibid., 163.

47. Larkin, *The Separation Issue*, 170.

48. Ibid., 209–11.

49. Ibid., 212.

50. McManners, *Church and State*, 169.

51. Ibid., 161–62.

52. Ibid., 109–10.

53. Mayeur, *Un Prêtre Démocrate*, 315.

54. Larkin, *The Separation Issue*, 161–62.

Chapter 2. Mobilization of French Priests

1. Martin, *Count Albert de Mun, Paladin of the Third Republic*, 290.

2. Brugerette, *Le prêtre française*, 3:361. He footnotes as witness to this statement, Mgr. Odelin, *L'Écho de Paris*, September 25, 1914.

3. Ibid., 356–357.

4. Fontana, *Les catholiques français*, 11–12, 45.

5. Philip Jenkins, *The Great and Holy War: How World War I Became a Religious Crusade* (New York: Harper One, 2014).

6. Fontana, *Les catholiques français*, 11–12.

7. These included several seminaries, the Institute Catholique in Toulouse, as well as the three-hundred-bed hospital in Lourdes. Ibid., 28–29.

8. Ibid., 72.

9. Ibid., 41

10. Ibid., 35–37.

11. Ibid., 38.

12. Pierre Lelièvre, *Le fléau de Dieu: Notes et impressions de guerre* (Paris: P. Ollendorff, 1920), 4.

13. J. M. Bourceret, *Sur les routes du front de Meuse: Souvenirs d'un infirmier-major* (Paris: Perrin, 1917), 4.

14. Brugerette, *Le prêtre française*, 3:371–72.

15. The French word *ambulance* throughout the text, unless otherwise specified, means the medical-surgical unit attached to an army corps or a division.

16. Bourceret, *Souvenirs d'un infirmier-major*, 96–97.

17. Paul Vigué, *Le sergent Pierre Babouard du 125e d'infanterie* (Paris: G. Beauchesne, 1917), 90–91.

18. Dominique Avon and Gérard Cholvy, *Paul Doncœur, S.J.*, 66. Avon specifies that this decree was referred to as Circulaire Malvy and is described more thoroughly in

"The Religious Orders in France, 1901–1945" by Nicholas Atkin, in Frank Tallett and Nicolas Atkin, *Religion, Society and Politics in France since 1789* (London: Hambledon Press, 1991).

19. Lelièvre, *Le fléau de Dieu*, 5.

20. Brugerette, *Le prêtre française*, 3:357–58.

21. Fontana, *Les catholiques français*, 30.

22. Achille Liénart and Catherine Masson, *La guerre de 1914–1918*, 17n7.

23. Soeur Christiane-Marie Decombe, Archiviste des soeurs de la Charité de Besançon, in "Synthèse de l'enquête sur le retour des Religieux en 14–18" (*Bulletin de l'Association des Archivistes de l'Église de France*, no. 74 [2010]: 22), presents the findings of a recent inquiry sent to 119 religious orders concerning the fate of members of their orders during and after World War I. She received just fifty-six responses. Among the questions she asked was one concerning the number of religious who had refused to return to France at the beginning of the war. There were no precise answers because of a lack of complete documentation. It was clear, however, that some stayed abroad due to the pressures from local ecclesiastical authorities who feared for the disorganization of their schools and other works. There was a less defined implication that others may have refused to return because they had previously been exiled.

24. Avon, *Paul Doncœur, S.J.*, 70. Avon provides no direct citation for this quotation from Bloy.

25. Fontana, *Les catholiques français*, 280; Larkin, *The Separation Issue*, 212; *La preuve du sang*, 1:xlv.

26. Fontana, *Les catholiques français*, 30.

27. Ibid., 284–85.

28. Annette Becker, *War and Faith*, 32–33; Michael Moynihan, *God on Our Side* (London: Secker & Warburg, 1983), 12.

29. Fontana, *Les catholiques français*, 285–86. A firsthand account is provided in Grandmaison and Veuillot, *L'aumônerie militaire*, xiv–xv. Also see Boniface, *L'aumônerie militaire français*, 68–69.

30. Fontana, *Les catholiques français*, 286.

31. Grandmaison and Veuillot, *L'aumônerie militaire*, 7.

32. Lelièvre, *Le fléau de Dieu*, 13–14.

33. Ibid., 20.

34. Liénart and Masson, *La guerre de 1914–1918*, 15–16.

35. Archives Historiques de l'Archevêché de Paris, Serie 5 B II 3. Abbé Ardant's war journal was written under the pseudonym Jean Limosin, and is referenced in this work.

36. Ibid.

37. Grandmaison and Veuillot, *L'aumônerie militaire*, 239.

38. Lelièvre, *Le fléau de Dieu*, 144, 147–48.

39. Boniface, *L'aumônerie militaire français*, 72–79.

40. Ibid., 71–72; Grandmaison and Veuillot, *L'aumônerie militaire*, 84–91, 102–3.

41. Grandmaison and Veuillot, *L'aumônerie militaire*, 216–18.

42. Ibid., 221.

43. Ibid., 223–24.

44. That dispensation is quoted in the 1914 letter to the archbishop of Paris. Archives Historiques de l'Archevêché de Paris, Serie 5 B II 13. Also, Fontana, *Les catholiques français*, 277–78. Although priests fighting in war is an anomaly in the modern era, Jonathan Riley-Smith reminds us in *The Crusades, Christianity, and Islam* (New York: Columbia University Press, 2008, 35), that after the first Crusade, professed religious, the brothers of military orders, were involved in warfare. Priests were encouraged to accompany armies to support soldiers in a spiritual manner in St. Thomas Aquinas's *Summa Theologiae*, written between 1267 and 1273. Thomas stressed, however, that priests were not permitted to carry arms. Also see David S. Bachrach, "The Friars Go to War: Mendicant Military Chaplains, 1216–c. 1300," *Catholic Historical Review* 90, no. 4 (2004), 621. Alain Toulza, in *La Grande Guerre des hommes de Dieu* (39) also refers to Aquinas's prohibition of the priest carrying arms but discusses in detail the changes in canon law. He states that canon law on this question was still being drafted during World War I. Ultimately it stated specifically that all priests were exempt from military service and that priests and seminarians will not volunteer to serve in the army without specific permission from their bishops. He states that St. Thomas never envisaged a general mobilization nor the principles of *laïcité*, but the catechism of the Catholic Church published in 1992 recognizes that governments can impose on all citizens the obligations necessary to national defense.

45. Fontana, *Les catholiques français*, 278–79.

46. Archives Historiques de l'Archevêché de Paris, Fonds Dubois, Serie 1 D XII 8. The main sources for Daniel Moulinet's book, *Prêtres soldats dans la Grande Guerre*, are letters of priests from the Diocese of Moulins who were mostly stretcher-bearers. Their correspondence is primarily with Abbé Arthur Sebastian Giraud, the superior of the seminary of Moulins.

47. Grandmaison and Veuillot, *L'aumônerie militaire*, 89; 82–83.

48. *Le Prêtre aux Armées*, no. 1, 15 février 1915, 1–2.

49. *Le Clergé de Paris aux Armées*, no. 1, juillet 1915, 1–5.

50. Ibid., no. 2, août 1915, 4.

51. A. Ménétrier, *Moine et soldat, le R. P. Édouard de Massat, 1860–1915* (Toulouse: Les Voix Franciscaines, 1918), 306–7.

52. *Bulletin Trimestriel des Anciens Élèves de Saint Sulpice*, nos. 76–77 (15 fevrier–15 mars, 1919), 87.

53. Grandmaison and Veuillot, *L'aumônerie militaire*, 31.

54. Ibid., 75.

55. Bourceret, *Souvenirs d'un infirmier-major*, 7.

56. Ibid., 25–26. "Manger du curé" or "To eat a curé" was an expression that had come to be used among anticlericals and Catholics alike for expressions of animosity toward the clergy.

57. Grandmaison and Veuillot, *L'aumônerie militaire*, 114. This same quote is cited in *La Croix*, October 3, 1914, column 1, p. 1.

58. See for example, *La Croix*, February 5, 1915. The list includes citations for nine priests, soldiers, stretcher-bearers, and chaplains.

59. *La Croix*, October 19, 1914.

60. Léonce Raffin, *Les carnets de guerre d'un prêtre-soldat, 1914–1918* (Paris: Bonne Presse, 1953), 227.

61. Pauline Beaufort, *L'âme héroïque d'un prêtre, Vie de l'abbé Jean Lagardère* (Besançon: Impr. Catholique de l'Est, 1928), 225.

62. Ibid., 227–31.

63. Ibid., 232.

64. Raffin, *Les carnets de guerre*, 228.

65. Archives Historiques de l'Archevêché de Paris, Serie 5 B II 3.

Chapter 3. Priests as Missionaries on the Battlefields

1. *La preuve du sang*, 1:xxi.

2. *La Croix*, October 19, 1914.

3. Max Caron, *Un lys brisé* (Paris: R. Haton, 1918), 102–3.

4. Ibid., 219–20.

5. Jean Nourisson, *Lettres de Jean Nourisson, aspirant au 153e régiment d'infanterie* (Paris: Gabalda, 1919), 12.

6. Ibid., 8.

7. Ibid., 17–18.

8. Ibid., 10.

9. P. L. Guichard, *Un jeune* (Paris: Librairie de l'Art Catholique, 1918), 58.

10. Font-Réaulx, *René de la Perraudière*, 36.

11. Xavier Thérésette and J. R. Jérôme, *Un moine soldat, Le sous-lieutenant Xavier Thérésette . . . en religion Fr. Marcel de Reims, OMC* (Paris: Gabriel Beauchesne, 1917), 58.

12. Anonymous, *Vaillant apôtre et vaillant capitaine, Le père Pierre Durouchoux, prêtre de la Companie de Jésus, capitaine au 274e d'infanterie* (Toulouse: Bureau de l'Apostolat de la Prière, 1918), 22.

13. Paul Tézenas du Montcel, *Dans les Tranchées: Journal d'un officier du 102e territorial (8 octobre 1914–2 avril 1917)* (Montbrison: Impr. E. Brassart, 1925), 46 and 59.

14. Jean Julien Weber and Jean-Noël Grandhomme, *Sur les pentes du Golgotha: Un prêtre dans les tranchées* (Strasbourg: Editions La Nué Bleu, 2001, 16), cites Jean Julien Weber, *Au soir d'une vie: Témoignages. Des remous du modernisme au renouveau conciliaire* (Paris: Le Centurion, 1972), 107. *Sur les pentes du Golgotha* was his war journal that he put together in two periods of convalescence during the war from his notebooks. He intended this only for family and friends as the story of his comings and goings and privations, but toward the end of his life gave permission for publication and editing by Grandhomme. The quotation here is from the memoir he published earlier, describing his entire life, entitled *Au soir d'une vie*.

15. Ibid., 17.

16. Ibid., cites Weber, *Au soir d'une vie*, 101.

17. Ibid., 49, cites Weber, *Au soir d'une vie*, 111.

18. Teilhard de Chardin, *The Making of a Mind*, 29.

19. Ibid., 26.

20. Ibid., 48.

21. Ibid., 51.

22. Bourceret, *Souvenirs d'un infirmier-major*, 7.

23. Ibid., 135.

24. Ibid., 136.

25. Liénart and Masson, *La guerre de 1914–1918*, 24.

26. Teilhard de Chardin, *The Making of a Mind*, 54.

27. Ibid., 83–84.

28. Ibid., 102.

29. Lud. Loiseau, *Un bon prêtre et un bon Français: L'Abbé Georges Sevin, curé d'Yèvre-la-Ville. Notes biographiques: Recuiellie par un de ses amis l'abbé Lud. Loiseau, professeur à l'école Saint-Grégoire de la Pithiviers* (Pithiviers: Impr. moderne, 1921), 113–14.

30. Albert Bessières, *Le chemin des dames, Carnet d'un territorial* (Paris: Bloud et Gay, 1918), 18–19.

31. Ménétrier, *Moine et soldat*, 262.

32. Georges Guitton, *Un "preneur" d'âmes: Louis Lenoir, aumônier des marsouins, 1914–1917* (Paris: J. de Gigord, Editeur, 1921), 51–56; and Georges Guitton and Georges Goyau, *Louis Lenoir, jésuite, aumônier militaire (1914–1918)* (Paris: Action Populaire, 1925), 11.

33. Guitton, *Louis Lenoir*, 18–19.

34. Frédéric de Bélinay, *Sur le sentier de la guerre* (Paris: Gabriel Beauchesne, 1920), 72–73.

35. Ibid., 73.

36. Cru, *Témoins*, 187.

37. Marcelin Lissorgues, *Notes d'un aumônier militaire* (Aurillac: Imp. Moderne, 1921), 16–17.

38. Liénart and Masson, *La guerre de 1914–1918*, 18–19.

39. Lelièvre, *Le fléau de Dieu*, 226–27.

40. Nourisson, *Lettres*, 115–23.

41. Ibid., 138.

42. Teilhard de Chardin, *The Making of a Mind*, 54.

43. Ibid., 174–75.

44. Bourceret, *Souvenirs d'un infirmier-major*, 184.

45. Ibid., 298.

46. Guitton, *Louis Lenoir*, 64.

47. Ibid., 66–67.

48. Ibid.

49. André de La Barre, *Une âme droite, André de la Barre de Carroy, aumônier militaire au 102e de ligne, . . . tué à Jonchery (Marne) le 26 juillet 1915* (Paris: Action Populaire, 1923), 116.

50. Ibid., 118.

51. Beaufort, *L'âme héroique d'un prêtre*, 170.

52. Ibid., 223.

53. Ibid., 201–2.

54. Her story is recounted by Raymond Jonas, *The Tragic Tale of Claire Ferchaud and the Great War* (Berkeley: University of California Press, 2005).

55. Lelièvre, *Le fléau de Dieu*, 252–53.

56. Liénart and Masson, *La guerre de 1914–1918*, 18–19.

57. Ibid., 63.

58. Raffin, *Les carnets de guerre*, 15.

Chapter 4. Priests as Patriots and Warriors

1. Feelings of comradeship and brotherhood were nearly universal among all the priests I studied. These were also commented on in the Catholic press. Daniel Moulinet's study of the letters of the priests from the Diocese of Moulins largely lacked such expressions. He commented on that fact, stating that perhaps the priests and seminarians hesitated to portray the "fraternity of the trenches" since their letters were directed to their superior. They tended to underline the differences between themselves and the other soldiers and emphasize religious realities. Moulinet, *Prêtres soldats dans la Grande Guerre*, 271–72.

2. *Nos prêtres ne sont pas des Embusqués*, February 29, 1916. Publication of the letters and account of the court proceedings Mgr. Quilliet, bishop of Limoges, brought against the newspaper, *Le Populaire du Centre*. Archives du Cardinal Dubois, *Situation des prêtres au front*, Archives Historique de l'Archevêché de Paris, 1D XII 8.

3. Teilhard de Chardin, *The Making of a Mind*, 24–26; 29.

4. Guichard, *Un jeune*, 40–41.

5. Bourceret, *Souvenirs d'un Infirmier-major*, 11–12.

6. Gabriel Chevoleau and Emile Bauman, *L'Abbé Chevoleau, Caporal au 90e infanterie* (Paris: Perin, 1917), 22–23.

7. Weber and Grandhomme, *Sur les pentes du Golgotha*, 16.

8. Thérésette and Jérôme, *Un moine soldat*, 40.

9. Caron, *Un lys brisé*, 127–28.

10. Font-Réaulx, *René de la Perraudière*, 41–42.

11. Guitton, *Un "preneur" d'âmes*, 113–14.

12. Bourceret, *Souvenirs d'un infirmier-major*, 201–2.

13. Guitton, *Un "preneur" d'âmes*, 311.

14. Teilhard de Chardin, *The Making of a Mind*, 170–71.

15. Raffin, *Les carnets de guerre*, 59–60.

16. Font-Réaulx, *René de la Perraudière*, 27.

17. René Gaëll, *Les soutanes sous la mitraille, scènes de la guerre* (Paris: Henri Gautier, 1915), 3–4.

18. Thérésette and Jérôme, *Un moine soldat*, 34–35; Cru, *Témoins*, 548.

19. *La preuve du sang*, 2:843.

20. Ibid., 1:712

21. Flagéat, *Les jésuites français*, 137.

22. Guitton, *Un "preneur" d'âmes*, 217–19.

23. Teilhard de Chardin, *The Making of a Mind*, 136.

24. Paul Dubrulle and Henry Bordeaux, *Mon régiment: Dans la fournaise de Verdun et dans la bataille de la Somme: Impressions de guerre d'un prêtre soldat* (Paris: Plon-Nourrit, 1917), 232–33.

25. Font-Réaulx, *René de la Perraudière*, 42.

26. Teilhard de Chardin, *The Making of a Mind*, 183.

27. Guitton, *Louis Lenoir*, 73–76.

28. Ducasse, *La guerre racontée*, 2:23.

29. Pierre Mayoux, *Paul Doncoeur, aumônier militaire* (Paris: Presses d'Ile de France, 1966), 69–71.

30. Chaline, "Les aumôniers catholiques," 100n11.

31. Teilhard de Chardin, *The Making of a Mind*, 194.

32. Ibid., 205.

33. Ibid., 206–7.

34. Guitton, *Louis Lenoir*, 82.

35. Beaufort, *L'âme héroïque d'un prêtre*, 203.

36. Ibid., 218.

37. Lelièvre, *Le fléau de Dieu*, 197.

38. Guitton, *Un "preneur" d'âmes*, 47.

39. Beaufort, *L'âme héroïque d'un prêtre*, 256–57.

40. Bourceret, *Souvenirs d'un infirmier-major*, 147–48.

41. Guitton, *Un "preneur" d'âmes*, 182.

42. Chevoleau and Bauman, *L'abbé Chevoleau*, 44–45.

43. Font-Réaulx, *René de la Perraudière*, 26.

44. Nourisson, *Lettres*, 54–55.

45. Caron, *Un lys brisé*, 181–83.

46. Lissorgues, *Notes d'un aumônier militaire*, 95, 145–48.

47. Liénart and Masson, *La guerre de 1914–1918*, 30.

48. Ibid., 42–43.

49. Bélinay, *Sur le sentier de la guerre*, 154–59.

50. Mayoux, *Paul Doncoeur*, 78.

51. Liénart and Masson, *La guerre de 1914–1918*, 43.

52. Guitton, *Un "preneur" d'âmes*, 173–74.

53. Ibid., 209.

54. Guitton, *Louis Lenoir*, 49–50.

55. Ibid., 193–94.

56. Riley-Smith, *The Crusades, Christianity, and Islam*, 31–33, 40. He traces the idea of penitential warfare to the First Crusade. The Crusades were seen as collective acts of penance. Pope John Paul II, in his Apostolic Letter of February 11, 1984, *Salvifici Doloris*, traced back to St. Paul the idea of the "salvific meaning" of suffering for

the remission of sins in union with Christ, quoting: "In my flesh I complete what is lacking in Christ's afflictions for the sake of his body, that is, the Church" (Col. 1, 24).

57. Ménétrier, *Moine et soldat*, 46–47; 259–60.

58. Charles Thellier de Poncheville, *Dix mois à Verdun* (Paris: J. de Gigord, 1919), 43.

59. Raffin, *Les carnets de guerre*, 149–50.

60. Teilhard de Chardin, *The Making of a Mind*, 92.

61. Font-Réaulx, *René de la Perraudière*, 43.

62. Caron, *Un lys brisé*, 283.

63. Stéphane Audoin-Rouzeau, "The National Sentiment of Soldiers during the Great War," in *Nationhood and Nationalism in France: From Boulangism to the Great War 1889–1918*, ed. Robert Tombs (New York: Harper Collins, 1991), 89–100.

Chapter 5. Priests as Military Pastors

1. Liénart and Masson, *La guerre de 1914–1918*, 16.

2. Teilhard de Chardin, *The Making of a Mind*, 50–51.

3. Jean Limosin [Georges-Maurice Ardant], *De Verdun à L'Yser: Notes d'un aumônier militaire* (Paris: Bonne Presse, 1917), 14.

4. Liénart and Masson, *La guerre de 1914–1918*, 32.

5. Ibid., 47.

6. Mayoux, *Paul Doncoeur*, 107.

7. Liénart and Masson, *La guerre de 1914–1918*, 23.

8. Ibid., 27.

9. Guitton, *Louis Lenoir*, 26–27.

10. Beaufort, *L'âme héroique d'un prêtre*, 241.

11. Caron, *Un lys brisé*, 219–20.

12. Nourisson, *Lettres*, 26–27.

13. Weber and Grandhomme, *Sur les pentes du Golgotha*, 177–78.

14. Raffin, *Les carnets de guerre*, 187–88.

15. Thellier de Poncheville, *Dix mois à Verdun*, 140.

16. Beaufort, *L'âme héroique d'un prêtre*, 257.

17. Ibid., 276 and *La preuve du sang*, 2:20.

18. Lissorgues, *Notes d'un aumônier militaire*, 95.

19. Ibid., 96–97.

20. Ibid., 25–26.

21. Lelièvre, *Le fléau de Dieu*, 218.

22. Liénart and Masson, *La guerre de 1914–1918*, 45–46.

23. Archives de l'armée de la terre, 1 K 284, no. 104, Fonds Veuillot, 1914–1919.

24. Ibid.

25. Ibid.

26. Grandmaison and Veuillot, *L'aumônerie militaire*, 58.

27. Ibid., 77.

28. Flagéat, *Les jésuites français*, 140.

29. Beaufort, *L'âme héroique d'un prêtre*, 206–7.

30. Grandmaison and Veuillot, *L'aumônerie militaire*, 66.

31. Limosin, *De Verdun à L'Yser*, 13–14.

32. Lelièvre, *Le fléau de Dieu*, 45.

33. Dubrulle and Bordeaux, *Mon régiment*, 15.

34. Thellier de Poncheville, *Dix mois à Verdun*, 115–16.

35. Lissorgues, *Notes d'un aumônier militaire*, 21.

36. Ibid., 19–20.

37. Bessières, *Carnet d'un territorial*, 68–69.

38. Lelièvre, *Le fléau de Dieu*, 132.

39. Chardin, *The Making of a Mind*, 142–43.

40. Flagéat, *Les jésuites français*, 119.

41. Weber and Grandhomme, *Sur les pentes du Golgotha*, 119.

42. Ibid., 119, and 302n52 cites Weber, *Au soir d'une vie*, 110–11.

43. Ibid., 135.

44. Ibid., 164.

45. Ibid., 176.

46. Georges Guitton, *Avec un régiment de l'Armée Gouraud le 415e d'infanterie: La poursuite victorieuse, 26 septembre–11 novembre 1918* (Paris: Payot, 1919).

47. Beaufort, *L'âme héroique d'un prêtre*, 217.

48. Bélinay, *Sur le sentier de la guerre*, 39.

49. Liénart and Masson, *La guerre de 1914–1918*, 37–38.

50. Ibid., 48.

51. Ibid., 86.

52. Limosin, *De Verdun à L'Yser*, 18.

53. Liénart and Masson, *La guerre de 1914–1918*, 39–40.

54. Ménétrier, *Moine et soldat*, 296.

55. Beaufort, *L'âme héroique d'un prêtre*, 211–12.

56. Lelièvre, *Le fléau de Dieu*, 222–23.

57. Georges Gaudy, *Les trous d'obus de Verdun* (Plon: 1922), 204–5, cited by Ducasse, *La guerre racontées*, 2:114–16.

58. Ducasse, *La guerre racontées*, 2:22.

59. Thellier de Poncheville, *Dix mois à Verdun*, 64–65.

60. Liénart and Masson, *La guerre de 1914–1918*, 48.

61. Flagéat, *Les jésuites français*, 199–200.

62. Annette Becker, *War and Faith*, 42–43.

Chapter 6. Memory of War in Postwar Relations

1. Sheldon Hackney, "The Initial Shock," A conversation with Paul Fussell, *Humanities* 17, no. 5 (1996): 9.

2. Beaufort, *L'âme héroique d'un prêtre*, 200, 203.

3. Ibid., 233.
4. Antoine Verriele, "Les Seminaristes de Saint-Sulpice Morts Pour La France," *Bulletin Trimestriel des Anciens Élèves de Saint Sulpice*, nos. 76–77 (15 fevrier–15 mars, 1919): 86–87.
5. Vigué, *Le sergent Pierre Babouard*, 100.
6. Thérésette and Jérôme, *Un moine soldat*, 48.
7. Bessières, *Carnet d'un territorial*, 118.
8. See Smith, *Embattled Self*; and Antoine Prost, *In the Wake of War: 'Les Anciens Combattants' and French Society*, trans. Helen McPhail (Providence, R.I.: Berg, 1992).
9. Prost, *In the Wake of War*, 24.
10. Ibid.
11. Ibid., 23.
12. Ibid., 26n67, which cites Tézenas du Montcel, *Dans les tranchées*, 394.
13. Vigué, *Le sergent Pierre Babouard*, 117.
14. L. G., *L'abbé Jean Audouin, clerc minoré, sergent au 135e d'infanterie* (Angers: Lecoq, 1917), 24.
15. Thellier de Poncheville, *Dix mois à Verdun*, 222.
16. Hackney, "The Initial Shock," 8. Jonathan H. Ebel's more recent work, *Faith in the Fight: Religion and the American Soldier in the Great War* (Princeton, N.J.: Princeton University Press, 2010) also refutes Fussell's more conventional view that the war proved more disillusioning to religious beliefs. Ebel provided examples of letters, diaries, and memoirs of American soldiers, nurses, and aid workers whose faith both encouraged them to fight and sustained them through the war's horrors.
17. Annette Becker, *War and Faith*, 11, 20–22. Psichari, a French writer, religious thinker, and soldier, was the grandson of Ernest Renan, author of *Life of Jesus*, which was condemned by Catholic authorities for its attempt at a critical treatment of Jesus as a human being. Psichari's conversion to Catholicism was much celebrated in the Catholic world. He died fighting in Belgium in August 1914. Henri Massis, a literary critic and essayist, was also a convert to Catholicism.
18. Philip Jenkins, *The Great and Holy War*, 29.
19. Archives de l'armée de la terre, Paris, 1 K 284, no. 104, Fonds Veuillot, 1914–1919.
20. Loiseau, *L'abbé Georges Sevin*, 87–89.
21. Liénart and Masson, *La guerre de 1914–1918*, 118.
22. Ibid., 8.
23. Bessières, *Carnet d'un territorial*, 77.
24. Teilhard de Chardin, *The Making of a Mind*, 264.
25. Ibid., 267–68.
26. Ibid., 272–73.
27. Flagéat, *Les jésuites français*, 453–56.
28. Ibid., 457.
29. *La preuve du sang*, 1:xli–xlii.
30. Ibid., 1:xliii–xliv.
31. Ibid., 1:xliv.

32. Ibid., 1:xlv.

33. *Semaine Religieuse de Dijon* (5 *août 1922*), 250–51, cited in Ibid., 1:li.

34. Dansette, *Under the Third Republic*, 333.

35. Ibid., 335.

36. Mayoux, *Paul Doncoeur*, 136.

37. Dansette, *Under the Third Republic*, 337–41.

38. Ibid., 345.

39. Annette Becker, *War and Faith*, 116–20.

40. Ibid.

41. Ibid., 173–74.

42. Le Moigne, "Groupes et individus dans l'episcopat français," 63.

43. Ibid., 53.

44. Ibid., 63.

45. Ibid.

46. Ibid.

47. Ibid., 60.

48. Liénart and Masson, *La guerre de 1914–1918*, 8.

49. Mayoux, *Paul Doncoeur*, 137.

50. Dansette, *Under the Third Republic*, 348.

51. Mayoux, *Paul Doncoeur*, 137.

52. Ibid.

53. Toulza, *La Grande Guerre des hommes de Dieu*, 138–39.

54. Dansette, *Under the Third Republic*, 349.

55. Ligue des Droits des Religieux Anciens Combattants DRAC 1924–1927, Archives Nationales, F/7/13228.

56. Ibid.

57. Ibid.

58. Ibid.

59. Raffin, *Les carnets de guerre*, 18–19.

60. Mayoux, *Paul Doncoeur*, 143.

BIBLIOGRAPHY

Archives

Archives de l'armée de la terre, Paris
 1 K 284, no. 104, Fonds Veuillot, 1914–1919
 1 K 284, no. 105, 1914–1918

Archives historiques de l'Archevêché de Paris
 Serie 1 D 11, 19. Archives du Cardinal Amette. Aumônerie de l'Armée de l'Orient à Salonique
 Serie 1 D XII 8. Archives du Cardinal Dubois. Prisonniers de guerre.
 Serie 5 B II.
  2 1914–1918: Aumônerie militaire. Vicariat aux Armées. Brochures.
  3 1914–1918: Prêtres aux armées; prisonniers; comité et œuvres de guerre
  4 1914–1918: Prêtres mobilisés (notamment à Salonique en 1917), correspondance
  7 1914–1918: Service Militaire du Clergé et dispenses
  11 1914–1918: Prisonniers de guerre, clergé pendant la guerre . . .
  12 1914–1918: Aumônerie militaire, séminaristes soldats, correspondance
  13 1914–1918: Ceremonies; la "Rumeur infâme"; divers
  14 1914–1918: Correspondance, réglementation canonique

Archives nationales, Paris
 Série F7 Police générale
  12 881 Catholicisme 1915–1916; 1918–1925.
  3 213 Mouvement catholique 1914–1917; 1924–1927.
  13 216 Notes et presse sur l'activité de la Ligue patriotique des Françaises 1910–1927.
  13 219 Fédération nationale catholique (FNC) 1924–1932.
  13 228 Ligue des droits des religieux anciens combattants (DRAC) 1924–1927.

Primary Sources

Anonymous. *Une fleur de saint abandon: Le P. Jean-Louis Dabo de la Congrégation de Jésus et Marie, sous-lieutenant de l'artillerie, tombé au Champ d'honneur, le 4 août 1917.* Besançon: Impr. Catholique de l'Est, 1917.

————. *Vaillant Apôtre et vaillant capitaine: Le père Pierre Durouchoux, prêtre de la Compagnie de Jésus, capitaine au 274e d'infanterie.* Toulouse: Bureau de l'Apostolat de la Prière, 1918.

Avon, Dominique, and Gérard Cholvy. *Paul Doncœur, S.J. (1880–1961): Un croisé dans le siècle.* Paris: Les Éditions du Cerf, 2001.

Beaufort, Pauline. *L'âme héroïque d'un pretre. Vie de l'abbé Jean Lagardère.* Besançon: Impr. Catholique de l'Est, 1928.

Bélinay, Frédéric de. *Sur le sentier de la guerre.* Paris: Gabriel Beauchesne, 1920.

Bessières, Albert. *Le Chemin des dames: Carnet d'un territorial.* Paris: Bloud et Gay, 1918.

Bordachar, Benjamin, and Maurice Feltin. *Un grand orateur: L'abbé Bergey, député de la Gironde, 1881–1950.* Paris: B. Grasset, 1963.

Bourceret, J. M. *Sur les routes du front de Meuse: Souvenirs d'un infirmier-major.* Paris: Perrin, 1917.

Bucaille, Victor. *Lettres de prêtres aux armées.* Paris: Payot, 1916.

Caron, Max. *Un lys brisé.* Paris: R. Haton, 1918.

Chevoleau, Gabriel, and Emile Bauman. *L'abbé Chevoleau, caporal au 90e d'infanterie.* Paris: Perrin, 1917.

Dubrulle, Paul, and Henry Bordeaux. *Mon régiment: Dans la fournaise de Verdun et dans la bataille de la Somme: Impressions de guerre d'un prêtre soldat.* Paris: Plon-Nourrit, 1917.

Font-Reaulx, André de. *René de la Perraudière, novice de la Compagnie de Jésus, sergent d'infanterie française, mort au champ d'honneur.* Toulouse: l'Apostolat de la prière, 1918.

Gaëll, René. *Les soutanes sous la mitraille, scènes de la guerre.* Paris: Henri Gautier, 1915.

Grandmaison, Geoffroy de, and François Veuillot. *L'aumônerie militaire pendant la guerre.* Paris: Bloud et Gay, 1923.

Grandmaison, Léonce de. *Impressions de guerre de prêtres soldats.* Paris: Plon-Nourrit, 1917.

Grivelet, Maurice. *Mémoires d'un curé: Fantassin, aviateur, resistant.* Is-sur-Tille: Robichon, 1970.

Guiard, Amedée. *Le carnet intime de guerre.* Paris: Bloud et Gay, 1918.

Guichard, P. L. *Un jeune.* Paris: Librairie de l'Art Catholique, 1918.

Guitton, Georges. *Avec un régiment de l'Armée Gouraud, le 415e d'infanterie: La poursuite victorieuse. 26 septembre–11 novembre, 1918.* Paris: Payot.1919.

————. *Un "preneur" d'âmes: Louis Lenoir, aumônier des marsouins, 1914–1917.* Paris: J. de Gigord, 1921.

Guitton, Georges, and Georges Goyau. *Louis Lenoir, jesuite, aumônier militaire (1914–1918).* Paris: Action Populaire, 1925.

Harel, Ambroise, and François Bertin. *Mémoires d'un poilu breton*. Rennes: Editions Ouest-France, 2009.

La Barre, André de. *Une âme droite: André de la Barre de Carroy . . . aumônier militaire au 102e de ligne, tué à Jonchery (Marne) le 26 juillet 1915*. Paris: Action Populaire, 1923.

Lelièvre, Pierre. *Le fléau de Dieu: Notes et impressions de guerre*. Paris: P. Ollendorff, 1920.

L. G. *L'abbé Jean Audouin, clerc minoré, sergent au 135e d'infanterie, mort pour la France le 6 septembre 1914*. Angers: Lecoq, 1917.

Liénart, Achille, and Catherine Masson. *La guerre de 1914–1918 vue par un aumônier militaire*. Villeneuve d'Ascq: Presses universitaires du Septentrion, 2008.

Limosin, Jean [Georges-Maurice Ardant, pseud.]. *De Verdun à l'Yser: Notes d'un aumônier militaire*. Paris: Bonne Presse, 1917.

Lissorgues, Marcelin. *Notes d'un aumônier militaire*. Aurillac: Imp. Moderne, 1921.

Loiseau, Lud. *Un bon prêtre et un bon Français, l'abbé Georges Sevin, curé d'Yèvre-la-Ville. Notes biographiques: Recueillie par un de ses amis l'abbé Lud. Loiseau*. Pithiviers: Impr. moderne, 1921.

Mayoux, Pierre. *Paul Doncoeur, aumônier militaire*. Paris: Presses d'Ile de France, 1966.

Ménétrier, A. *Moine et soldat: Le R. P. Édouard de Massat, 1860–1915*. Toulouse: Les Voix Franciscaines, 1918.

Mugnier, Arthur, Marcel Billot, and Jean d'Hendecourt. *Journal de l'abbé Mugnier: 1879–1939*. Paris: Mercure de France, 1985.

Nourisson, Jean. *Lettres de Jean Nourisson, aspirant au 153e régiment d'infanterie*. Paris: Gabalda, 1919.

Raffin, Léonce. *Les carnets de guerre d'un prêtre-soldat, 1914–1918*. Paris: Bonne Presse, 1954.

Sainte-Pierre, Dominique, ed. *La Grande Guerre entre les lignes: Correspondances, journaux intimes et photographies de la famille Saint-Pierre, réunis et annotés*. 2 vols. Bourg-en-Bresse: Musnier-Gilbert Éditions, 2006.

Schuhler, J. *Ceux du 1er Corps. Souvenirs, impressions, récits de la guerre par un aumônier militaire*. 2nd ed. Colmar: Les Éditions D'Alsace, 1932.

Teilhard de Chardin, Pierre. *The Making of a Mind: Letters from a Soldier Priest, 1914–1919*. Translated by René Hague. New York: Harper and Row, 1965.

Tézenas du Montcel, Paul. *Dans les Tranchées. Journal d'un officier du 102e territorial (8 octobre 1914–2 avril 1917)*. Montbrison: Impr. E. Brassart, 1925.

Thellier de Poncheville, Charles. *Dix mois à Verdun*. Paris: J. de Gigord, 1919.

Thérésette, Xavier, and J. R. Jérôme. *Un moine soldat: Le sous-lieutenant Thérésette . . . en religion Fr. Marcel de Reims, OMC*. Paris: Gabriel Beauchesne, 1917.

Vigué, Paul. *Le sergent Pierre Babouard du 125e d'infanterie*. Paris: G. Beauchesne, 1917.

Weber, Jean Julien, and Jean Noël Grandhomme. *Sur les pentes du Golgotha: Un prêtre dans les tranchées*. Strasbourg: Nuée Bleu, 2001.

Periodicals

Bulletin Trimestriel des Anciens Élèves de Saint-Sulpice, 1914–18

La Croix, 1914, 1915, 1926

Le Clergé de Paris aux Armées, Correspondance Diocésaine, 1915–18
Le Prêtre aux Armées. Bulletin bimensuel des prêtres et des religieux mobilisés, 1915
La Semaine religieuse de Paris, 1915

Secondary Sources

Acomb, Evelyn M. *The French Laic Laws (1879–1889): The First Anti-Clerical Campaign of the Third French Republic*. New York: Columbia University Press, 1941.

Audoin-Rouzeau, Stéphane. *Men at War, 1914–1918: National Sentiment and Trench Journalism in France during the First World War*. Oxford: Berg, 1992.

Audoin-Rouzeau, Stéphane, and Annette Becker. *14–18, retrouver la guerre*. Paris: Gallimard, 2000.

Bach, André. "Le citoyen-soldat: Entre consentement et coercion." In Cazals, *La Grande Guerre*, 321–330.

Becker, Annette. *War and Faith: The Religious Imagination in France, 1914–1930*. Translated by Helen McPhail. Oxford: Berg, 1998.

Becker, Jean-Jacques. *Histoire Culturelle de la Grande Guerre*. Paris: A. Colin, 2005.

Becker, Jean-Jacques, and Stéphane Audoin-Rouzeau. *Les sociétés européennes et la guerre de 1914–1918: Actes du colloque organisé à Nanterre et à Amiens du 8 au 11 décembre 1988*. Nanterre: Publications de l'Université de Nanterre, 1990.

Beirnaert, Michel. "La Preuve du sang, Livre d'or du clergé et des congrégations, 1914–1922," *Bulletin de l'Association des Archivistes de l'Église de France*, no. 74 (2010): 40–43.

Bengy, Marie-Hélène de. " Les congrégations religieuses féminines impliquées dans la guerre 1914–1918." *Bulletin de l'Association des Archivistes de l'Église de France*, no. 74 (2010): 28–39.

Boniface, Xavier. *L'aumônerie militaire française, 1914–1962*. Paris: Cerf, 2001.

———. "L'aumônerie militaire française, 1914–1962." PhD thesis, University of Lille, 1992.

Brown, Frederick. *For the Soul of France: Culture Wars in the Age of Dreyfus*. New York: Alfred A. Knopf, 2010.

Brugerette, Joseph. *Le prêtre français et la société contemporaine*. Vol. 2, *Vers la séparation de l'église et de l'état (1871–1908)*, and Vol. 3, *Sous le régime de la séparation, la reconstitution catholique, 1908–1936*. Paris: P. Léthielleux, 1938.

Byrnes, Joseph. "The Limits of Personal Reconciliation: Priests and *Instituteurs* in World War I." In *Catholic and French Forever: Religious and National Identity in Modern France*. University Park: Pennsylvania State University Press, 2005.

Carrard, Philippe. *The French Who Fought for Hitler: Memories from the Outcasts*. New York: Cambridge University Press, 2010.

Cazals, Rémy, Emmanuelle Picard, and Denis Rolland, eds. *La Grande Guerre: Pratiques et expériences*. Toulouse: Privat, 2005.

Chaline, Nadine-Josette, ed. *Chretiens dans la premiere guerre mondiale*. Paris: Cerf, 1993.

Chrastil, Rachel. *Organizing for War: France 1870–1914*. Baton Rouge: Louisiana State University Press, 2010.

Clark, Christopher, and Wolfram Kaiser. *Culture Wars: Secular-Catholic Conflict in Nineteenth-Century Europe*. Cambridge, UK: Cambridge University Press, 2003.

Coffey, Joan L. "The Aix Affair of 1891: A Turning Point in Church-State Relations before the Separation?" *French Historical Studies* 21, no. 4 (1998): 543–59.

———. "For God and France: The Military Law of 1889 and the Soldiers of Saint-Sulpice." *Catholic Historical Review* 88, no. 4 (2002): 679–701.

Crerar, Duff. *Padres in No Man's Land: Canadian Chaplains in the Great War.* Montréal: McGill-Queen's Press, 1995.

Cru, Jean Norton. *Témoins: Essai d'analyse et de critique des souvenirs de combattants édités en français de 1915 à 1928.* Paris: Les Etincelles, 1929.

Dansette, Adrien. *Religious History of Modern France.* Vol. 2, *Under the Third Republic.* New York: Herder and Herder, 1961.

Darrow, Margaret H. "Volunteer Nursing and the Myth of the War Experience." *American Historical Review* 101, no. 1 (1996): 80–106.

Decombe, Christiane-Marie. "Synthèse de l'enquête sur le retour des Religieux en 14–18." *Bulletin de l'Association des Archivistes de l'Église de France*, no. 74 (2010): 18–27.

Ducasse, André. *La guerre racontée par les combattants: Anthologie des écrivains du front (1914–1918).* Paris: E. Flammarion, 1932.

Duroselle, Jean-Baptiste. *La Grande Guerre des français, 1914–1918: L'incompréhensible.* Paris: Perrin, 2002. First published in 1994.

Ebel, Jonathan H. *Faith in the Fight: Religion and the American Soldier in the Great War.* Princeton, N.J.: Princeton University Press, 2010.

Flagéat, Marie-Claude. *Les jésuites français dans la Grande Guerre, témoins, victimes, héros, apôtres.* Paris: Cerf, 2008.

Fontana, Jacques. *Les catholiques français pendant la Grande Guerre.* Paris: Cerf, 1990.

Fouilloux, Étienne. "Première Guerre Mondiale et Changement Religieux en France." In Becker, *Histoire culturelle de la Grande Guerre*, 115–24.

Fussell, Paul. *The Great War and Modern Memory.* London: Oxford University Press, 1977.

Hackney, Sheldon. "The Initial Shock." A conversation with Paul Fussell. *Humanities* 17, no. 5 (1996): 4–9.

Hanna, Martha. *The Mobilization of Intellect: French Scholars and Writers during the Great War.* Cambridge, Mass.: Harvard University Press, 1996.

———. *Your Death Would Be Mine: Paul and Marie Pireaud in the Great War.* Cambridge, Mass.: Harvard University Press, 2006.

Hardier, Thierry. "Les chapelles souterraines." In Cazals, *La Grande Guerre*, 355–64.

Higonnet, Margaret R., ed. *Nurses at the Front: Writing the Wounds of the Great War.* Boston: Northeastern University Press, 2001.

Hochschild, Adam. *To End All Wars: A Story of Loyalty and Rebellion, 1914–1918.* Boston: Houghton Mifflin Harcourt, 2011.

Jenkins, Philip. *The Great and Holy War: How World War I Became a Religious Crusade.* New York: Harper One, 2014.

Jonas, Raymond. *The Tragic Tale of Claire Ferchaud and the Great War.* Berkeley: University of California Press, 2005.

Kale, Steven D. *Legitimism and the Reconstruction of French Society, 1852–1883.* Baton Rouge: Louisiana State University Press, 1992.

Kselman, Thomas. "Challenging Dechristianization: The Historiography of Religion in Modern France." *Church History* 75, no. 1 (2006): 130–39.

———. *Miracles and Prophecies in Nineteeth-Century France.* New Brunswick, N.J.: Rutgers University Press, 1983.

Lalouette, Jacqueline. *La libre pensée en France, 1848–1940.* Paris: Albin Michel, 1997.

———. *La république anticléricale XIXe-XXe siècles.* Paris: Éditions du Seuil, 2002.

Larkin, Maurice. *Church and State after the Dreyfus Affair: The Separation Issue in France.* New York: Harper and Row: 1973.

Latreille, André, Étienne Delaruelle, Jean Rémy Palanque, and René Rémond. *Histoire du catholicisme en France.* Vol. 3, *La période contemporaine.* Paris: Éditions Spes, 1962.

Le Bon, Gustave. *Psychology of the Great War: The First World War and Its Origins.* New Brunswick, New Jersey: Transaction Publishers, 1999. First published in 1916. With an introduction by Martha Hanna and a foreword by Irving Louis Horowitz.

Le Moigne, Frédéric. "Groupes et individus dans l'épiscopat français au milieu du vingtième siècle (1930–1950)." PhD diss., Université de Rennes 2, 2000.

McManners, John. *Church and State in France, 1870–1914.* New York: Harper & Row, 1972.

Martin, Benjamin F. *Count Albert de Mun, Paladin of the Third Republic.* Chapel Hill: University of North Carolina Press, 1978.

May, Anita Rasi. "The Falloux Law, the Catholic Press, and the Bishops: Crisis of Authority in the French Church." *French Historical Studies* 8, no. 1 (1973): 77–94.

Mayeur, Jean Marie. *Un prêtre démocrate: L'abbé Lemire, 1853–1928.* Paris-Tournai: Casterman, 1968.

Mosse, George. *Fallen Soldiers: Reshaping the Memory of the World Wars.* New York: Oxford University Press, 1990.

———. "Two World Wars and the Myth of the War Experience." *Journal of Contemporary History* 21, no. 4, (1986): 491–513.

Moulinet, Daniel. *Prêtres soldats dans la Grande Guerre: Les clercs bourbonnais sous les drapeaux.* Rennes: Presses Universitaire de Rennes, 2014.

Moynihan, Michael. *God on Our Side.* London: Secker & Warburg, 1983.

Mueller, Olaf. "*Le Feu* de Barbusse: La 'vraie bible' des poilus. Histoire de sa reception avant et après 1918." In Cazals, *La Grande Guerre*, 131–40.

Nye, Robert A. *Masculinity and Male Codes of Honor in Modern France.* New York: Oxford University Press, 1993.

———. *The Origins of Crowd Psychology: Gustave Le Bon and the Crisis of Mass Democracy in the Third Republic.* London: Sage Publications, 1975.

Pappola, Fabrice, and Alexandre Lafon. "'Bourrage de crânes' et expériences combattantes." In Cazals, *La Grande Guerre*, 311–20.

Pascal, Jean. *Les ecclésiastiques parlementaires français, 1848–1977.* Pontoise: Edijac, 1988.

La Preuve du Sang: Livre d'or du clergé et des congrégations, 1914–1922. 2 vols. Paris: Bonne Presse, 1925–1930. Available online at: https://dioceseauxarmees.fr/la-preuve-du-sang-le-livre-d-or.html.

Prost, Antoine. *In the Wake of War: 'Les Anciens Combattants' and French Society.* Translated by Helen McPhail. Oxford: Berg, 1992.

Rémond, Réne. *L'anticlericalisme en France, de 1815 à nos jours.* Paris: Fayard, revised and augmented edition, 1999. (3rd version.) First published in 1976.

———. *The Right Wing in France: From 1815 to de Gaulle.* Translated by James M. Laux. Second and revised edition. Philadelphia: University of Pennsylvania Press, 1969. First published in 1966.

Riley-Smith, Jonathan. *The Crusades, Christianity, and Islam.* New York: Columbia University Press, 2008.

Rotundo, E. Anthony. *American Manhood: Transformations in Masculinity from the Revolution to the Modern Era.* New York: Basic Books, 1993.

Saunders, Nicholas J. *Matters of Conflict: Material Culture, Memory and the First World War.* London: Routledge, 2004.

Schweitzer, Richard. *The Cross and the Trenches: Religious Faith and Doubt among British and American Great War Soldiers.* Westport, Conn.: Praeger Publishers, 2003.

Scott, Joan Wallach. *The Politics of the Veil.* Princeton, N.J.: Princeton University Press, 2007.

Sherman, Daniel J. "Objects of Memory: History and Narrative in French War Museums." *French Historical Studies* 19 (1995): 49–74.

Smith, Leonard V. *Embattled Self: French Soldier Testimony of the Great War.* Ithaca, N.Y.: Cornell University Press, 2008.

———. "Jean Norton Cru et la subjectivité de l'objectivité." In Becker, *Histoire culturelle de la Grande Guerre,* 89–100.

Smith, Leonard V., Stéphane Audoin-Rouzeau, and Annette Becker. *France and the Great War, 1914–1918.* French sections translated by Helen McPhail. Cambridge, UK: Cambridge University Press, 2003.

Tombs, Robert, ed. *Nationhood and Nationalism in France: From Boulangism to the Great War 1889–1918.* London: Harper Collins, 1991.

Toulza, Alain. *La Grande Guerre des hommes de Dieu: Héros des tranchées, entre persécutions et Union sacrée.* Paris: DRAC, 2015.

Weber, Eugen. *Peasants into Frenchmen: The Modernization of Rural France, 1870–1914.* Stanford: Stanford University Press, 1976.

Winter, Jay. *Remembering War: The Great War between Memory and History in the Twentieth Century.* New Haven, Conn.: Yale University Press, 2006.

Zeldin, Theodore, ed. *Conflicts in French Society: Anticlericalism, Education, and Morals in the Nineteenth Century.* London: George Allen and Unwin: 1970.

Zeldin, Theodore. *France 1848–1945.* Vol. 2. *Intellect, Taste, and Anxiety.* Oxford: Clarendon Press, 1977.

INDEX

Pius IX (pope), 13
Pius X (pope), 23, 119
Poincaré, Raymond, 27, 117–18
postwar experiences of priests. *See*
priests, veteran
priests: 1880–81 expulsion of, 16–18;
conscription of, 3, 5, 18–19, 31–33; in
exile, 21, 32, 137n23; and monarchical
government, 12, 133n4; prewar
relationship with secular society, 5,
8–10; pro-clerical laws, 12–13; religious
orders of, 9, 20–21, 23, 119, 122, 129;
religious pilgrimage by, 13–14, 134n11.
See also anticlerical laws; religion
priests, veteran: leagues for, 115, 123;
postwar comradeship of, 10, 109,
111–12, 115–16; postwar memory
projects on, 114–17; postwar protests
with, 102, 123–25, 129
priests, wartime, 8–10, 127–30; on
battlefield engagement, 73–76, 80;
on battlefield nostalgia, 76–78; on
battlefield strategies, 81–83; and
bravery, 73, 85, 97–98, 103, 127; burial
services by, 102–3, 104, 107, 108;
challenges of, 35–36; combatant and
noncombatant assignments of, 37–38;
communication of, 89, 94–96, 107,
108; on corrupting influences, 47;
criticism and suspension of, 43–45;
discipline of, 43, 45, 66, 72, 74, 128;
disillusionment of, 112–13; historical
examples of, 138n44; on horrors of
war, 78–79, 93–94, 132n7; lack of
pacifism among, 29, 66, 78, 79–80;
memorial masses by, 106–7; military
conscription laws for, 3, 5, 18–19,
31–33; military *vs.* religious sacrifice
of, 84–88, 142n56; mobilization of,
28–29, 31–32; on morality of war, 6,
27–29, 66, 80–82, 113; organization of,
5, 33–37; patriotism of, 9, 27–29, 65,
111; poetic appreciation for, 104–5; in

praise of soldiers, 97–101; promotions
of, 32, 37–38, 41, 72–73; published
stories of, 5–8, 67, 131n6, 132n7, 132n13;
reception by lay commanders of, 38,
43, 57–58, 64, 66, 128; reception by
soldiers of, 42–43, 46–48; reception of
secular society of, 29–30; recollections
of, 50–52, 56–57, 56–60; on soldier
conversions and piety, 61–62; total
number of, 8, 32, 46, 67, 117, 121;
wartime comradeship of, 9–10, 53,
66–67, 110–11, 128. *See also* chaplains,
wartime; pastoral duties, wartime
Principes de la guerre (Foch), 74
pro-clerical laws, 11, 12–13
Prost, Antoine, 111–12
protest demonstrations, 102, 123–25, 129
Psichari, Ernest, 113, 145n17

Quilliet, Hector-Raphael, 67–68

Raffin, Léonce: on meaning of war,
86–87; military service of, 43, 86;
on obedience, 72; pastoral duties
by, 92–93; published stories of, 7; on
reception of wartime priests, 44, 65;
on union sacrée, 125–26
reading rooms, 42
reconciliation, postwar, 113–16, 118–21
Red Cross. *See* Croix Rouge
religion, 8–26; 1896 proposed reforms,
24–25; canon laws, 3, 18, 138n44;
and "culture wars," 11, 133n1, 134n8;
education in, 12, 14, 15–17, 20, 21–22,
135n20; effects of modernization on, 15;
fear of cultural feminization by, 6; and
fiscal management, 14, 22–24, 134n13;
laws against (*See* anticlerical laws); on
meaning of war, 9, 85–86, 111–13, 128;
pilgrimages, 13–14, 134n11; postwar
reconciliation of state and, 113–16,
118–21; prewar relationship with
secular society, 5, 8–10; pro-clerical